CAMPAIGN 311

SAVANNAH 1779

The British turn south

**SCOTT MARTIN AND
BERNARD F. HARRIS JR,**

ILLUSTRATED BY GRAHAM TURNER

Series editor Marcus Cowper

Osprey Publishing
c/o Bloomsbury Publishing Plc
PO Box 883, Oxford, OX1 9PL, UK

E-mail: info@ospreypublishing.com

www.ospreypublishing.com

OSPREY is a trademark of Osprey Publishing Ltd, a division of Bloomsbury Publishing Plc.

First published in Great Britain in 2017

© 2017 Osprey Publishing Ltd

All rights reserved. No part of this publication may be used or reproduced in any form, without prior written permission, except in the case of brief quotations embodied in critical articles and reviews. Inquiries should be addressed to the Publisher.

A CIP catalog record for this book is available from the British Library.

ISBN: PB: 9781472818652
ePub: 9781472818676
ePDF: 9781472818669
XML: 9781472822734

17 18 19 20 21   10 9 8 7 6 5 4 3 2 1

Index by Alison Worthington
Typeset in Myriad Pro and Sabon
Maps by Bounford.com
3D BEVs by The Black Spot
Page layouts by PDQ Digital Media Solutions, Bungay, UK
Printed in China through World Print Ltd.

ARTIST'S NOTE

Readers may care to note that the original paintings from which the colour plates in this book were prepared are available for private sale. All reproduction copyright whatsoever is retained by the Publishers. All enquiries should be addressed to:

Graham Turner, PO Box 568, Aylesbury, Buckinghamshire, HP17 8ZX
www.studio88.co.uk

The Publishers regret that they can enter into no correspondence upon this matter.

Osprey Publishing supports the Woodland Trust, the UK's leading woodland conservation charity. Between 2014 and 2018 our donations are being spent on their Centenary Woods project in the UK.

To find out more about our authors and books visit www.ospreypublishing.com. Here you will find extracts, author interviews, details of forthcoming events and the option to sign up for our newsletter.

DEDICATION

Scott Martin: this book is dedicated to my family – Kris, Douglas and Mallory – for their support and inspiration.

Bernard F. Harris Jr: this book is dedicated to my family – Opal, Patricia, Moselle, Shirley and Wayne.

ACKNOWLEDGMENTS

Scott would like to thank the Georgia Coastal Heritage Society: Nora, Emily, Aaron, and Ray for their support and for serving as gracious hosts during his visit to Savannah; to Arthur at Fort Morris Historic Site; and especially to Rhonda for her patience and technical support.

Bernard would like to thank his friends Alex and Rhonda for their technical support, Marcus Cowper of Ilios Publishing, and the many other organizations which assisted him with compiling the images for this book.

CONTENTS

THE STRATEGIC SITUATION	5
CHRONOLOGY	8
OPPOSING COMMANDERS	10
American commanders . French commanders . British commanders	
OPPOSING FORCES	16
American forces . French forces . British forces . Orders of battle	
OPPOSING PLANS	25
American plans . French plans . British plans	
THE CAMPAIGN	33
Midway . Sunbury . Capture of Savannah . Expedition to Augusta . Battle of Kettle Creek Battle of Brier Creek . Expedition to Charles Town . Battle of Stono Ferry . The French arrive Siege . Bombardment . Attack on the Spring Hill redoubt	
AFTERMATH	89
THE BATTLEFIELD TODAY	91
FURTHER READING	93
INDEX	95

THE STRATEGIC SITUATION

In 1778 Great Britain set in motion a series of events, which led to a renewed British southern strategy focus in the American Revolutionary War. Unlike the first invasion in 1776, which left British hopes of a speedy end to the conflict in shambles on the fields of North Carolina, this time there was the firm belief that southern Loyalists were waiting for the opportunity to flock to the King's colors and that a potentially weaker colonial defense would give the British hope for a different outcome. However, in February 1778 the war expanded and shifted into a global conflict.

This new threat was brought about by French King Louis XVI's decision to support the American cause and become an active player in the war. The threat of an expanding worldwide conflict gave momentum to King George III and his ministers to work with Parliament and meet the former demands of the colonists, thereby repealing the Tea Act and most of the Intolerable Acts under the assumption and hope that hostilities in North America would end. To propose this renewed peace effort, Lord Carlisle led a peace commission to America. However, in case the peace effort was unsuccessful, the British Government urged George Sackville (Lord Germain), the British Secretary of State for the American Colonies, to instruct Lieutenant-General Henry Clinton, Commander of British military forces in North America to achieve two objectives. The first objective was to bring General George Washington's northern army to a decisive battle. If this was unsuccessful by October 1778, the second objective was to shift his efforts south and move against Georgia and South Carolina. In the summer of 1778, General Clinton pulled his army out of Philadelphia in two columns and withdrew across New Jersey. General Washington's army emerged from Valley Forge with a new-found professional spirit and confidence, and in late June 1778 it fought the British to a standstill. The battle of Monmouth Courthouse was the last large-scale battle in the northern states. As Clinton's army settled into its New York City encampments, Clinton focused on his second objective to the south and looked to the capture of Savannah, the capital and largest seaport of Georgia.

Founded in 1733, Savannah is situated on a 40ft-high bluff overlooking the Savannah River to its north and 18 miles inland from the Atlantic Ocean. Although roads existed connecting Savannah with other towns in Georgia, the network of navigable rivers and network of waterways along the coast made water transportation easier, faster, cheaper, and safer. Plank-built schooners and sail craft were commonly used to transport goods along the inland waterways.

Portrait of Louis XVI, King of France and Navarre (1754–93), by Antoine-François Callet, displayed in the Palace of Versailles. (Universal History Archive/UIG via Getty Images)

February 6, 1778 French King Louis XVI officially recognizes the United States, represented by Benjamin Franklin, as an independent nation. (Robert Sears, Pictorial History of the American Revolution)

Fig. 158.—Acknowledgment of American Independence by France.

The pre-revolution population of Georgia numbered 30,000 people, with almost half being slaves. The colony was located on a narrow strip of land 40 to 50 miles in width, running west along the Savannah River and along the Georgia coastline. By 1775, Savannah's population exceeded 3,000 citizens, most living in 450 wooden houses situated on bluffs overlooking the river. The cash crop for the Georgia colonial economy was rice and cultivated by 20–25 rice plantations in and around Savannah and the coast. In 1751, the Georgia Colonial Charter changed to allow slavery. Africans from the marshy rice-cultivating coast of West Africa were especially valued because of their experience in the complicated and labor-intensive process of growing rice. In addition to Savannah and Augusta, separated by 120 miles, Sunbury was the other strategic town and seaport of entry. The city was 30 miles south of Savannah, and was Georgia's second port, boasting about 800 residents. In 1764, Sunbury contained at least 80 dwellings on a high bluff overlooking the wharves on the Medway River to its north. The other inland strategic town in Georgia was Ebenezer, located along the Savannah River

Savannah, Georgia was the last colonial capital established. The unique city design was laid out by General James Oglethorpe, who created a repeated pattern of connected neighborhoods, multiple squares, streets, and common (park) areas to enable city growth. (Robert Sears, Pictorial History of the American Revolution)

Fig. 135.—Savannah, 1778.

Charles Town, home to 12,000 residents and the fourth largest city in America. The city served as the economic center for commerce in the southern colonies, exporting rice, indigo, and cotton. In August 1783, the city became known as Charleston. (Library of Congress)

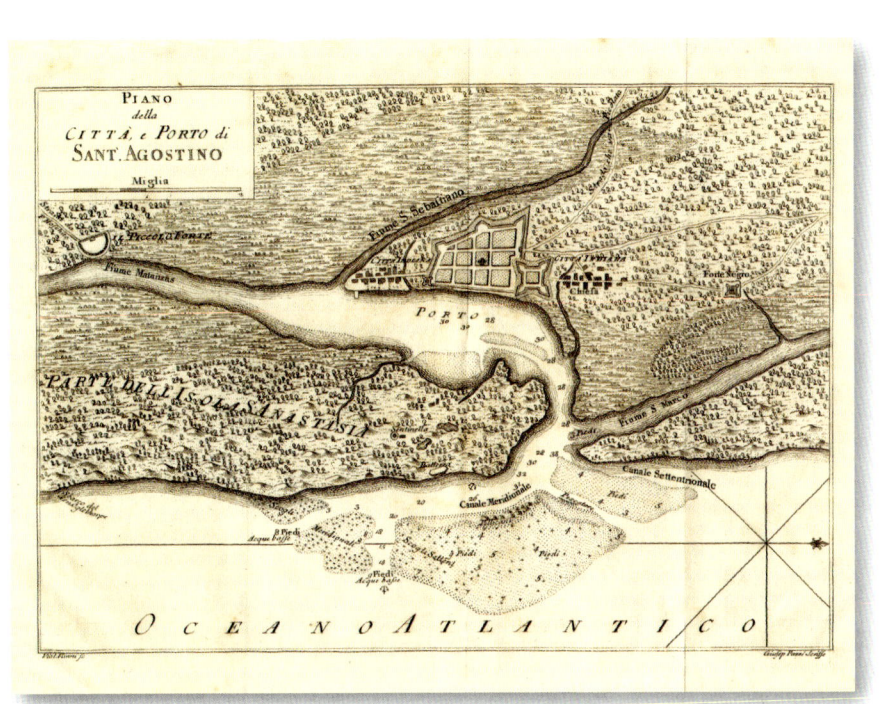

and with a pre-Revolution population of 500 residents, many of whom were German and Scottish immigrants. The town of Augusta was known as the center of Native American trade in the southeast and had 1,000 people living in 100 houses in the town and surrounding area. The strongest and most numerous Native American tribe in the southeast was the Cherokee Nation, other tribes included the Creeks, Choctaw and Seminoles.

St Augustine, capital of East Florida and a safe haven for Loyalist families evicted from their homes in Georgia and South Carolina by their Patriot neighbors. (State Library of Florida)

CHRONOLOGY

1775

April 20	Siege of Boston begins
December 9	Battle of Great Bridge, VA, American victory
December 31	Battle of Quebec, British victory

1776

February 27	Battle of Moore's Creek, NC, American victory
March 3	Battle of the Rice Boats, Savannah, GA, British victory
March 17	British evacuate Boston, MA
June 28	British bombardment of Fort Sullivan, SC, American victory
July	Cherokees attack along the frontier from Virginia to Georgia
July 4	Declaration of Independence
September 15	British capture New York City
December 25	Battle of Trenton, NJ, American victory

1777

January 2	Battle of Princeton, NJ, American victory
May 20	Treaty with Cherokees, American victory
September 26	British capture Philadelphia, PA
October 8	British Army surrenders at Saratoga, NY

1778

February 6	France signs secret treaty with the United States
March 8	Lieutenant-General Sir Henry Clinton appointed commander-in-chief of all British forces in North America
May 4	Continental Congress ratifies treaty with France
June 18	British evacuate Philadelphia, PA
June 28	Battle of Monmouth, NJ, British tactical victory
December 23	British land at Tybee Island, GA
December 29	British capture Savannah, GA

1779

January 31	British forces occupy Augusta, GA
February 3	Battle of Port Royal Island, SC, American victory
February 14	Battle of Kettle Creek, GA, American victory
March 3	Battle of Brier Creek, GA, British victory
June 19	French capture St Vincent
June 20	Battle of Stono Ferry, SC, British victory
June 21	Spain declares war on Britain
July 4	French capture Grenada

September 23	American/French forces begin siege of Savannah
October 3	French begin bombardment of Savannah
October 9	Battle of Savannah, British victory

1780

February 11 to May 11	British begin siege of Charles Town (Charleston), SC
May 12	American army surrenders at Charles Town
May 29	Battle of Waxhaws, SC, British victory
August 16	Battle of Camden, SC, British victory
October 7	Battle of King's Mountain, SC, American victory

1781

January 17	Battle of Cowpens, SC, American victory
March 15	Battle of Guilford Courthouse, NC, British tactical victory
May 10	Spanish capture Pensacola, FL
October 19	British Army surrenders at Yorktown, VA

1782

July 11	British depart Savannah
November 30	First peace treaty signed in Paris, France
December 14	British evacuate Charles Town

OPPOSING COMMANDERS

AMERICAN COMMANDERS

Major-General Robert Howe (1732–86) was educated in England, joined the North Carolina militia in 1764. He was commander of the 2nd North Carolina Regiment and participated in the British defeat at Great Bridge east of Norfolk, Virginia on December 9, 1775. For his service, Colonel Howe was promoted to brigadier-general in the Continental Army in March 1776 and assigned to the southern command under the command of Major-General Charles Lee. In September 1776, Congress approved his appointment to the rank of major-general and he was given command of the southern department. He personally directed the third expedition to capture St Augustine in British East Florida but experienced, first hand, the difficulties of leading a mixed force of Continental regulars along with state militias over which he had no direct authority. His last action in the Southern Department was his costly decision to defend Savannah on December 29, 1778.

Major-General Benjamin Lincoln (1733–1810) was 5ft 9in. tall, with a broad stature and heavy set, who suffered from a speech impediment and narcolepsy; he was known to fall asleep at the most inopportune times. A deeply religious man, he and Mary Cushing, his wife of 54 years, raised 11 children during their marriage. He began the war as a lieutenant-colonel in a Massachusetts militia and, because of his leadership and administrative skills, quickly rose to the rank of major-general following the New York 1776 campaign. At the battle of Saratoga (Bemis Heights) on October 7, 1777, a British musket ball shattered his right ankle. After a year's recovery, he returned to active duty in August 1778 and reported to General Washington's headquarters at White Plains, NY. The Continental Congress soon selected him as the strong and confident leader it needed to command and reorganize the Southern Department.

Brigadier-General William Moultrie (1730–1805) was given the commission of colonel in the 2nd South Carolina Regiment on June 17, 1775. Later as commander of the fort and garrison on Sullivan Island, he repelled a British naval bombardment and an attack in June 1776. He earned national recognition and the

Major-General Robert Howe, as the Southern Department commander, was constantly challenged by the Georgia and South Carolina assemblies to evict the British from East Florida. His decision to defend Savannah led to the destruction of his army and reputation. (State Archives of North Carolina)

Major-General Benjamin Lincoln was one of the three American commanders to be honored for the victory at Saratoga. In September 1778, he was selected by the Continental Congress to lead the Southern Department. (National Archives)

rank of brigadier-general in the Continental Army for his defense actions. Moreover, the fort was named Fort Moultrie in his honor. In May 1779 as the military commander of Charles Town defenses, he refused to surrender the city to Major-General Augustine Prevost. A year later, he was captured following the siege of Charles Town and remained imprisoned for the next two years. He was exchanged for British Major-General John Burgoyne in February 1782 and finished the war as a major-general.

Brigadier-General Isaac Huger (1742–97) was selected as a lieutenant-colonel for the 1st South Carolina Continental Regiment, and later promoted to colonel of the 5th South Carolina Continental Regiment in 1776. His brigade participated in the defense of Savannah. He was commissioned a brigadier-general in the Continental Army on January 9, 1779 and was wounded during the battle of Stono Ferry. He led the militia attack on the British left flank during the attack on Savannah. He served in the Southern Department throughout the war.

Brigadier-General Count Casimir Pulaski (1747–79) was born in Poland and, while in France, he befriended Benjamin Franklin to support the colonial cause. In 1777, he arrived in America not speaking any English, and communicated through interpreters speaking French. Congress made

RIGHT
Brigadier-General William Moultrie, as the senior South Carolina Continental officer, served as General Lincoln's second in command throughout 1779. (National Archives)

FAR RIGHT
Colonel Casmir Pulaski befriended Benjamin Franklin while in Paris. Franklin sent a letter of recommendation to General Washington, describing Pulaski as "an Officer famous throughout Europe for his Bravery and Conduct in Defense of the Liberties of his Country against the three great armies." He is commonly referred to as the father of the United States Cavalry. (National Archives)

Vice Admiral D'Estaing, following the defeat at Savannah, returned to France where he received a hero's welcome in Paris. Although he never returned to America, he would remain a staunch supporter of the revolution and strongly argued for a second expedition to America. (National Archives)

him a brigadier-general and saw his first action at Brandywine Creek and Germantown. By a Congress resolution on March 28, 1778, he was authorized to raise "an independent corps of 68 horse and 200 men." On November 10, 1778 the Pulaski legion was detached from Washington's main army and sent to serve under Lincoln's command. His legion provided much-needed intelligence of the British positions around Stono Ferry in May and June 1779. He was wounded during the assault on the Spring Hill redoubt and was evacuated onboard the brig *Wasp* for transport to Charles Town, but died two days later.

FRENCH COMMANDERS

Vice Admiral Charles-Henri, Count d'Estaing (1729–94), a celebrated French general and commander of Toulon, France, was appointed as the naval officer to take command of the French fleet departing Toulon for America. Unable to attack the British in New York City, he sailed north and attempted an unsuccessful combined operation with American forces to take Newport, Rhode Island. Severe weather off the coast and an intervention by a stronger British fleet off the Rhode Island coast forced d'Estaing to withdraw his fleet. The American commanders at Newport, Generals John Sullivan and John Stark, were outraged and came just short of calling d'Estaing a coward for his withdrawal. Although his ego was bruised, d'Estaing sailed for the Caribbean in November 1778 and led successful operations in the West Indies before sailing north to Georgia. Following the defeat at Savannah, d'Estaing and part of his fleet returned to France. His staunch support for the American cause propelled the second French expedition under the command of Count de Rochambeau. Unfortunately, Madame Guillotine killed this patriot to the American cause during the French Revolution.

BRITISH COMMANDERS

George Sackville, Lord Germain (1716–85), succeeded Lord Dartmouth as Secretary of State for the American Colonies in November 1775 and would remain in office throughout the war. He managed and directed the war effort over 3,000 miles away, which led to his eventual loss of favor within the British Administration and Court as the war continued, as well as with the powerful English merchants. Influenced by strong encouragement from the former Royal Governors of Virginia, Carolinas, and Georgia, along with the stalemate in the northern American colonies, Germain directed the war to shift toward the southern colonies.

Lieutenant-General Sir Henry Clinton (1739–1812) became General Howe's second in command during the 1776 New York campaign following his unsuccessful attack on Fort Sullivan. Appointed as the Commander-in-Chief of the British forces in North America, he relieved General Howe in Philadelphia and withdrew the Army from Philadelphia to New York fighting the June 28, 1778 inconclusive battle of Monmouth Courthouse, New Jersey. As a result of the news of France declaring war against Great Britain, he was forced to detach a number of regiments from his command to strengthen the garrisons in various British-held islands in the Caribbean and British West Florida (Pensacola, Florida). As the summer of 1778 came to a close, Clinton was in a stalemate position with no visible signs of defeating Washington's Continental army and was getting pressure from Britain to shift his attentions southward where the belief was that a strong loyalist support was just waiting for the opportunity to rally around the King's colors. Germain would conclude in one of his correspondences to Clinton, "I have thus stated the King's wishes and intentions, but he does not mean you to look upon them as orders, desiring ... that you use your discretion in planning ... all operations which shall appear the most likely means of crushing the rebellion." He agreed with Lord Germain's decision to shift the war effort to the southern colonies.

Sir James Wright (1716–85) was an attorney and plantation owner, he served as Royal Governor of Georgia since April 1761. A successful and respected governor, he encouraged the colony's growth by attracting new settlers, successfully negotiated with the Native Americans and oversaw the expansion of Georgia's western territory into the back-country. Wright himself became one of the largest landowners in Georgia with 11 plantations and 523 slaves. As the revolutionary fervor spread throughout the colonies in the early 1770s, Wright's

Lieutenant-General Sir Henry Clinton agreed to Lord Germain's decision to shift the war effort to the southern colonies. He sent an expedition to capture Savannah to serve as a staging base in the south for future operations. (Library of Congress)

BELOW LEFT
Royal Governor Sir James Wright was a successful and respected governor of Georgia. He encouraged the colony's growth by attracting new settlers, successfully negotiated with the Native Americans and oversaw the expansion of Georgia's western territory. He was the only Royal Governor to return to his colonial state and restore Royal law during the course of the war. (Dave Gilcreast and Georgia Historical Society)

BELOW RIGHT
Major-General Prevost, known as "bullet head" after a musket ball wounded his left temple during the British capture of Quebec in 1759. As the senior military commander in East Florida, he was promoted to brigadier-general, effective on April 1, 1777, "to act in the rank of Brigadier-General so long as the latter continued to serve in North American continent" to ensure his rank was senior to East Florida Governor, Patrick Tonyn, who held a reserve rank of colonel. (State Archives of Florida)

popularity, along with his administrative ability, effectively delayed the rebellious activity in Georgia. He was placed under house arrest, and eventually escaped onboard HMS *Scarborough*.

Following the British capture of Savannah in December 1778, Wright returned to the city on July 22, 1779. He quickly established himself as the reinstated Royal Governor and rescinded all laws going back to 1775, essentially ending the established American government in Georgia. He brought with him an entire staff of supporters and justices of the courts who governed Georgia until July 1782. His son, Major James Wright, commanded the Georgia Loyalists during the siege of Savannah.

Major-General Augustine Prevost (1723–86) was born in Geneva, Switzerland and served in the 60th (Royal American) Regiment of Foot during the French and Indian War. He was known as "bullet head" after a musket-ball wound in his temple during the capture of Quebec in 1759. Prevost united with Campbell's expeditionary force in Savannah and took command of all British forces in Georgia and was promoted to major-general in February 1779. Campbell wrote about his first impression of Prevost, "a worthy man, but too old and unactive for service. He will do in Garrison."

Lieutenant-Colonel Archibald Campbell (1739–91) began his military career in the British Army as an engineer and was wounded during the siege of Quebec in 1759. Following the French and Indian War, he served in the British East India Company's Bengal Engineers. At the outbreak of the American Revolution, Campbell was commissioned a lieutenant-colonel of the 71st Foot but was captured outside of Boston. In November 1778, Campbell, with no field experience in America, was appointed by General Clinton to lead the expedition to Georgia.

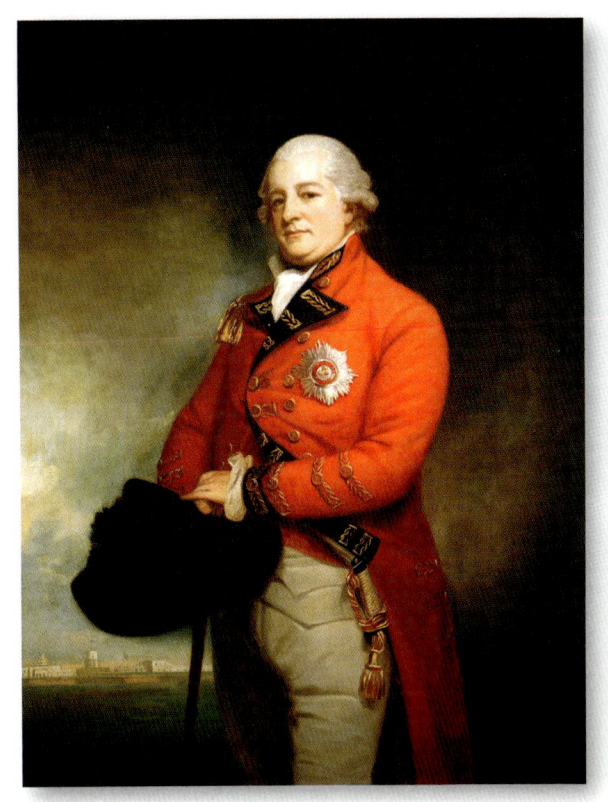

He wrote in his journal about his disappointment at not being promoted to brigadier-general, an appropriate rank for the responsibilities he would shoulder as leader of the expedition. Officers senior in rank to Campbell protested about him being promoted ahead of them and Clinton gave in to them. Campbell further noted, "Although I felt myself greatly disappointed in not obtaining the Rank promised me, yet the Reflection of commanding 3000 Men, and of having an Opportunity of exerting myself in the Service of my King and Country overbalanced every other Consideration." His expedition captured Savannah and Augusta. He departed for Britain on March 13, 1779, having turned his command over to Lieutenant-Colonel James Prevost, younger brother to General Prevost.

Lieutenant-Colonel John Maitland (1732–79). He was assigned to the 71st Regiment in October 1778, to serve as commander of the 1st Battalion and given command of the regiment during the Savannah expedition. He earned the respect of the 71st, as well as of his American adversaries, both in the northern and southern theaters. He was infected with malaria during the 1779 summer campaign along the South Carolina coast and died from it following the battle of Savannah. As noted by one historian, "His has been the fate of most British heroes of the American Revolution – unrecognized in this country, forgotten at home."

Captain James Moncrief (1741–93), a Scottish Highlander and graduate of the Royal Military Academy. He served as a royal engineer throughout his career. He participated in Britain's conquest of Spanish Florida in 1763 and won notoriety after developing a detailed map of St Augustine. He served in the 1777 Philadelphia campaign and was instrumental as the chief engineer responsible for building the Savannah defenses.

ABOVE LEFT
Lieutenant-Colonel Archibald Campbell was captured along with several companies of the 71st Highland Regiment, shortly after the British abandoned Boston, but unknown to the ship carrying them as they entered Boston harbor. He was eventually exchanged for Ethan Allen in May 1778. Campbell's first command in America was the expedition to Savannah. (National Gallery of Art)

ABOVE RIGHT
Lieutenant-Colonel John Maitland (1732 to October 25, 1779) served as a Royal Marine officer during the Seven Years War, when he lost his right hand. He was a battalion commander and then commander of the 71st Regiment in 1778–79. Suffering from malaria during the summer of 1779, he led his force to reinforce the defenses of Savannah. He died of malaria shortly after the defense of Savannah. (The Maitland Trust Fund)

OPPOSING FORCES

AMERICAN FORCES

Prior to the British shift in strategy to focus on the southern colonies, the American army of the Southern Department had been plagued with recruitment, clothing, food, pay, and equipment challenges. Many of the regiments serving along the coast from Charles Town to Sunbury spent many idle days on garrison duty and this, coupled with sickness, eroded their fighting spirit. Although their militia along the Georgia–East Florida border and in the back-country were more on constant alert for Tory rangers and Indian incursions, many of the men would then retire back home after the threat went away. Moreover, the rift of command between Major-General Robert Howe and the colonial governors of Georgia and South Carolina was a source of constant friction, especially following each of the three unsuccessful attempts by the Southern Department to capture British-controlled East Florida.

Continental
The Continental regiments of Georgia and South Carolina had, by December 1778, little combat experience compared with the British and Loyalist units fighting against General Washington's northern army. The South Carolina war experience was limited to the aborted British naval attack on Sullivan Island in June 1776. The defense of Fort Sullivan by the 2nd South Carolina regiment under Colonel Moultrie elevated his regiment to the status of an elite regiment within the state. However since then, all of the regiment's recruiting efforts to fill the ranks were a chronic challenge, many of the able-bodied men not wanting to fall under the Continental Army orders and regulations. To support the southern governors, the Continental Congress granted permission for those states to recruit men from North Carolina to Pennsylvania in an attempt to augment their regiments to full strength. Each company was authorized to consist of up to 62 men to include officers. These recruiting efforts would later create tension between these southern and northern governors.

The four Georgia Continental regiments were organized into eight companies each and formed the Georgia Brigade. The 2nd Georgia was initially organized in Williamsburg, Virginia and along with the 1st Georgia served under Colonel Samuel Elbert during the second expedition to East Florida. The 3rd Regiment was raised in North Carolina and served along the Georgia coast from Savannah to New Brunswick. The 4th Regiment was organized near Philadelphia, Pennsylvania and assigned to the Georgia Brigade in December 1777. All four regiments participated in the third expedition to capture East Florida. By April 1779, the Brigade could muster only 98 men fit for duty because of the arduous campaigning along the Georgia coastal swamps, sickness, desertions, battle casualties, and capture. Moreover, to counter the Tory raiders based out of East Florida, the independent Georgia Regiment of Horse Rangers grew from four to 12 troops by January 1777 and served throughout Georgia. In the fall of 1776, Georgia created two Continental artillery companies to serve along the Georgia coastline. The 1st company was captured at Savannah on December 29, 1778 and the 2nd was captured on January 10, 1779 at Sunbury.

The 4th and 5th North Carolina Regiments served under General Washington but suffered severely at Valley Forge and were later re-organized and assigned to the Southern Department, serving under Colonel Armstrong's North Carolina brigade at the battle of Stono Ferry.

The 1st and 2nd South Carolina Regiments organized into ten separate companies in November 1775, from men in eastern South Carolina. The 1st Regiment participated in the third expedition to East Florida and both regiments defended Charles Town (1779). The 3rd Regiment organized into nine companies in July 1776 from men in western South Carolina. The 4th Artillery Regiment was organized in December 1775 at Charles Town and participated in the defenses of Fort Sullivan (1776) to the siege of Savannah in 1779. The 5th Regiment organized into even companies in February 1776 from men in eastern and northern South Carolina. The 3rd, 4th, and 5th served in the South Carolina Brigade under the command of Colonel Isaac Huger during the defense of Savannah.

Typical uniform of a Georgia Continental soldier. (New York Historical Society)

Georgia and South Carolina Patriot militia

The militia units from each state were commanded by their respective governors and assigned to a respective brigade commander from their districts. The main reason for their volunteering to serve was to protect their homes from marauding Indian bands and incursions from the Loyalists operating from

17

The French Charleville smoothbore musket was one of the primary weapons for the American and French soldier. It fired a .69-caliber bullet and was 76 inches long when mounted with a socket bayonet. A well-trained soldier could fire three aimed shots in one minute. (National Archives)

East Florida. Campbell wrote to General Clinton on March 4, 1779 about the Georgia and South Carolina militia his expedition encountered, "The Time of their Nine Months men is almost expired, and every Circumstance shews [shows], that they are not fond of encountering the regular Troops." As noted by Campbell, the quality of the leadership and fighting spirit varied greatly between each unit. His experience, mainly against the Georgia militia, reinforced his position with regard to the unreliability of the rebel militia. Campbell would have had a different opinion if he had encountered the South Carolina Ninety-Six militia regiment, commanded by Colonel Andrew Pickens. It was a veteran unit, having participated in numerous conflicts with Native Americans in the back-country and was one of the units participating at Kettle Creek. Moreover, when properly led, clothed, and trained, the militia formed a respectable force as noted by d'Estaing in his impression of the Charles Town grenadiers and militia in September 1779.

FRENCH FORCES

Following the Seven Years War, the French Army restructured its organizations. By 1776, French regiments consisted of two battalions comprising six companies. These companies consisted of four fusilier, one grenadier and one chasseur (light) companies. At full strength each regiment comprised 963 officers and men; however, on active service it rarely achieved its full complement of men, on account of sickness and injuries. The colonial

FAR LEFT
The French Gatinois Regiment participated in the siege of Savannah and later participated in the Yorktown, Virginia campaign. (New York Historical Society)

LEFT
Uniform of the Chasseurs-Volontaires de Saint-Domingue, a 540-man volunteer force of free Africans, many former slaves recruited in Santo Domingo. The regiment was attached to the reserve column during the October 9 assault. (Coastal Heritage Society)

battalions were recruited, many from the various islands, and organized with a grenadier, chasseur and eight line companies for a total strength of 750 men. By the summer of 1779, the French regiments would have been wearing an assortment of uniform jackets between the 1776 short jacket and the February 1779 regulation white long-tail jacket with white turnbacks ornamented with lilies for fusilier, grenades for grenadiers, and bugle horns for chasseur companies. The new 1779 uniform would have slowly been phased into the regiments, especially for the metropolitan (from France) regiments deployed overseas. An eyewitness to d'Estaing's July 1779 attack on Grenada noted French soldiers with white coats and long tails and white turnbacks. Dillon's Irish regiment was noted as wearing a short red coat with yellow turnbacks. The following regiments at Savannah would be considered metropolitan: Armagnac, Auxerrios (captured Grenada), Agenois, Cambresis (captured Grenada), Champagne (captured St Vincent, grenadiers captured Grenada), Gatinois, Hainault (grenadiers captured Grenada), Foix (captured Grenada and left a detachment to garrison the island) and Viennois (captured St Vincent, grenadiers captured Grenada).

The two foreign (Irish) regiments in red jackets comprised expatriates from Ireland and original descendants who had fled Ireland 90 years earlier. Dillon's regiment had yellow facing and participated in the capture of Grenada; Walsh's regiment had blue facings.

BRITISH FORCES

British Regulars
The majority of the British line formations that captured Savannah and remained to conduct operations in Georgia and southern South Carolina were Scottish and German mercenaries. The core of the British force consisted

RIGHT
Although the 71st Highland Regiment was recruited from the Scottish Highlands, the men did not wear the kilt, but wore standard white breeches. (Coastal Heritage Society)

FAR RIGHT
Typical Royal Marine uniform. The marines were transferred from several British ships bottled up on the Savannah River and distributed to augment the city defenses. (Coastal Heritage Society)

Von Trumbach Hessian uniform. Lieutenant-Colonel Campbell in his diary referred to the von Trumbach Regiment as Welworth, his spelling based on the regiment's previous commander von Woellwarth. (Coastal Heritage Society)

of two battalions of the 71st Highland (Fraser Highlander) Regiment, except their Grenadier companies which stayed in New York. The 71st was raised in 1775 in Scotland; it was the first British regiment to be raised after the start of the war. The 71st distinguished itself in a number of campaigns in and around New York City from August 1776 to Brandywine Creek in 1777.

Lieutenant-Colonel Campbell augmented his expedition with a cavalry (dragoon) force, composed of 50 men selected from the 71st Regiment to serve as dragoons under the command of Lieutenant Thomas Tawes. He referred to Tawes as a gallant and experienced officer, and promoted him to captain. Campbell wrote in his journal that he was indebted to his friend and the zeal of Sir William Erskine, Quartermaster General at New York for giving him 50 suits (jackets) of cavalry accoutrements. The jackets were adjusted to fit the 50 men during their transit from New York to Savannah.

The other British line regiments that marched north from St Augustine, Florida were the 60th Regiment, the majority of which were German, and several companies of the 16th Regiment of Foot. The standard equipment for the men weighed 63lb, which consisted of the Brown Bess musket that weighed 11lb 7oz, a coat that weighed 5lb 2oz, a knapsack that weighed 7lb 10oz and contained two shirts, three pairs of socks, two pairs of stockings, one pair of summer breeches, one pair of shoes, brushes and six rations, all weighing 39lb.

The German (Hessian) troops

One of the two German regiments, Campbell referred to them in his journal as battalions, that captured Savannah and defended it during the September–October siege was the von Trumbach Regiment. Originally named the Rall Regiment after its commander, the regiment was nearly

Two of the three DeLancy loyalist battalions were sent on the expedition to Savannah. The battalions garrisoned a number of outposts along the Savannah River following the capture of Savannah and participated in General Prevost's expedition to Charles Town. (New York Historical Society)

annihilated at the battle of Trenton, December 1776. The survivors of the regiment were reconstituted and designated von Woellwarth in 1777 and eventually named von Trumbach in 1778. The regiment would remain in the Savannah and Charles Town area until the winter of 1782–83. The other Hessian battalion was von Wissenbach, both regiments were from Hesse-Cassel. The Hessian regiments were named after their regimental commanders and both regiments had served in the northern theater since the summer of 1776.

Loyalists with Campbell's expedition

DeLancey's Brigade, also known as the New York Loyalists, was composed of three battalions of 500 men and was raised by Oliver DeLancy, a wealthy New York merchant. The 1st and 2nd battalions served under Campbell's expedition. Prior to their departure the 1st and 2nd battalions changed their green uniforms to brick-red wool with green facings. DeLancy stayed with his 3rd Battalion in New York.

The 3rd Battalion of New Jersey Volunteers was formed in November 1776 and served in Georgia until 1782 when it returned to Long Island. The 3rd was one of four New Jersey Loyalist volunteer battalions raised by Cortland Skinner, the last royal attorney general of New Jersey. Skinner provided his four battalions with green uniforms, a color that came to be associated with armed Tories. However, in 1778 the British Government decided to clothe Provincials in red jackets, based on the regimental stores of those regiments ordered home (10th, 46th, and 52nd). Waistcoats and breeches were white except in those regiments with buff facings.

East Florida Rangers

The East Florida Rangers were raised along the Georgia–Florida border, primarily from East Florida, and included Loyalists driven from their homes in Georgia and South Carolina by Patriots. The rangers staged harassment raids throughout Georgia, especially between St Marys River up to Savannah. Their operations and the question of who commanded them caused considerable tension between the East Florida Royal Governor Patrick Tonyn and General Prevost. Under their militia commander, Lieutenant-Colonel Thomas Brown, they proved to be formidable opponents throughout the war. Tonyn commissioned him as a lieutenant-colonel. Brown was nicknamed "Burnfoot" by a lynch mob of anti-government rebels. Brown had recently migrated to Georgia from England in 1774 and became one of many Tory victims to suffer at the hands of the Patriots for not denouncing the King. He was attacked by a mob of 100 back-country Georgians near his home at Augusta. They tied him to a tree, beat and kicked him until he lost consciousness, and then scorched his feet with hot irons, which cost him two toes. A reported eyewitness described the scene, "They burnt his feet, tarred and cut his hair."

In May 1779 Governor Tonyn wrote to Prevost that the East Florida Rangers were no longer considered attached to East Florida and recommended that they be taken into the King's service. Prevost reconstituted them into a provincial regiment of infantry under the name of King's Rangers and recommended the officers hold a provincial rank. When East Florida was returned to Spain, as per the 1783 peace treaty, Brown and several of his rangers and their families settled in the Bahamas.

ORDERS OF BATTLE

BATTLE OF SAVANNAH, DECEMBER 29, 1778

AMERICAN FORCES: MAJOR-GENERAL ROBERT HOWE

South Carolina Brigade, Colonel Isaac Huger
    5th South Carolina Continental Regiment, Colonel Isaac Huger (169 men)
    3rd South Carolina Rangers, Lieutenant-Colonel William Thompson (295 men)
Georgia Brigade, Colonel Samuel Elbert (200 men)
Georgia Militia, Colonel George Walton (100 men)
City of Savannah Militia at Savannah Fort (50 men)
4th South Carolina Artillery, Colonel Owen Roberts (40 men)
9 x 4lb cannons
American Total: 854 men and 9 cannons

BRITISH FORCES: LIEUTENANT-COLONEL ARCHIBALD CAMPBELL

71st Regiment, Lieutenant-Colonel John Maitland
    1st Battalion (437 men)
    2nd Battalion (507 men)
Light Infantry Corps
    Light Infantry Company, Captain Sir James Baird (184 men)
    Light Infantry Company, Captain Charles Cameron (170 men)
Hessian Regiment von Woellwarth, Lieutenant-Colonel von Kettle (442 men)
Hessian Regiment von Wissenbach, Lieutenant-Colonel Friedrich von Porbeck (448 men)
New York Volunteers, Lieutenant-Colonel George Turnbull (234 men)
DeLancy's New York Regiment
    1st Battalion (219 men)
    2nd Battalion (160 men)
Cortland Skinner's New Jersey Regiment, 3rd Battalion (242 men)
8 x 3lb cannons (36 men)
British Total: 3,079 men and 8 cannons

BATTLE OF BRIER CREEK, MARCH 3, 1779

AMERICAN FORCES: BRIGADIER-GENERAL JOHN ASHE

North Carolina Militia Brigade: Brigadier-General Bryan (800 men)
    New Bern Regiment
    Halifax Regiment, Colonel Eaton
    Wilmington Regiment
    Edenton Regiment, Colonel Perkins
    Georgia Continentals, Brigadier-General Samuel Elbert (70 men)
    North Carolina Light Infantry, Lieutenant-Colonel Anthony Lytle (200 men)
Light horse detachment (40 men)
1 x 4lb and 2 x 2lb cannons
Total: 1,110 men and 3 cannons

BRITISH FORCES: LIEUTENANT-COLONEL JAMES PREVOST

2nd Battalion, 71st Regiment, (400 men), Lieutenant-Colonel John Maitland
Light Infantry Corps, Captain Sir James Baird (299 men)
Grenadier Corps of Florida Brigade, Major Beamsly Glazier (100 men)
Light Dragoons, Captain Thomas Tawes (42 men)
Carolina provincials (150 men)
2 x 6lb and 2 x 3lb cannons (20 men)
1 x 5.5in. howitzer (5 men)
Total: 1,016 men and 5 cannons

BATTLE OF STONO FERRY (SOUTH CAROLINA, JUNE 20, 1779)

AMERICAN FORCES: MAJOR-GENERAL BENJAMIN LINCOLN

Left Wing: Brigadier-General Isaac Huger
2nd Battalion Light Infantry, Lieutenant-Colonel John Henderson (115 men)
South Carolina Brigade: Colonel William Thompson
    1st South Carolina Continental Regiment, Colonel Charles Pinckney (215 men)
    3rd South Carolina Continental Regiment, Col William Thompson (402 men)
    6th South Carolina Continental Regiment, Lieutenant-Colonel William Henderson (164 men)
North Carolina Continental Brigade: Colonel James Armstrong
    4th North Carolina Continental Regiment, Lieutenant-Colonel James Thackston (282 men)
    5th North Carolina Continental Regiment, Colonel James Armstrong (315 men)
4th South Carolina Artillery (4 x 4lb guns), Colonel Owen Roberts (26 men)
Right Wing: Brigadier-General Jethro Sumner
1st Battalion light Infantry, Colonel Francis Malmady (358 men)
South Carolina Militia Brigade, General Andrew Williamson (417 men)
North Carolina Militia Brigade, General John Butler (400 men)
4th South Carolina Artillery detachment (2 x 4lb guns, 12 men)
Reserve
Virginia Militia Brigade, Colonel David Mason (283 men)
South Carolina Horse, Lieutenant-Colonel Daniel Horry (50 men)
4th South Carolina Artillery detachment (2 x 4lb guns, 12 men)
Total: 3,051 men and 8 cannons

BRITISH FORCES: LIEUTENANT-COLONEL JOHN MAITLAND

1st Battalion, 71st Regiment, Major Duncan McPherson (350 men)
Hessian Regiment von Wissenbach (200 men)
Provincials, Lieutenant-Colonel John Hamilton (250 men)
    North Carolina Volunteers
    1st Battalion South Carolina Royalists
2 x 6lb and 5 x 3lb cannons
1 x 5.5in. howitzer
Total: 800 men and 6 cannons

BATTLE OF SAVANNAH, OCTOBER 9, 1779

AMERICAN FORCES: MAJOR-GENERAL BENJAMIN LINCOLN

Advance Guard (cavalry): Brigadier-General Count Casimir Pulaski
Pulaski Legion (125 men)
1st Regiment Virginia Light Dragoons, Major John Jameson (166 men)
South Carolina Light Dragoons, Lieutenant-Colonel Daniel Horry (50 men)
Right Column: Lieutenant-Colonel John Laurens
Lieutenant-Colonel John Laurens' Light Corps
Corps of Light Infantry (190 men)

Grenadier Company, Charles Town militia (50 men)
2nd South Carolina Continental Regiment, Colonel Francis Marion (166 men)
3rd South Carolina Continental Regiment, Colonel William Thompson (210 men)
1st Virginia Continental Levies, Colonel Richard Parker (166 men)
1st Battalion, Charles Town militia, Colonel Maurice Simons (206 men)
Left Column: Brigadier-General Lachlan McIntosh
1st South Carolina Continental Regiment, Colonel Charles Pinckney (125 men)
5th South Carolina Continental Regiment, Lieutenant-Colonel Alexander McIntosh (166 men)
6th South Carolina Continental Regiment, Lieutenant-Colonel William Henderson (103 men)
Brigadier-General Isaac Huger's Column
Georgia and South Carolina Militia (500 men)
Reserve
4th South Carolina Artillery, Colonel Barnard Beekman (101 men)
8 x 4lb cannons
2 x 6lb cannons
American Total: 3,155 men and 10 cannons

FRENCH FORCES: VICE ADMIRAL HENRI COUNT D'ESTAING

Vanguard of the Army, Colonel Jules Bethisy
Volunteer Grenadier Company, Captain Aubrey (60 men)
Volunteer Grenadier Company, Captain Herneville (60 men)
Volunteer Grenadier Company, Captain De Veone (60 men)
Grenadier Company of Armagnac (49 men)
Chasseur Company of Armagnac (53 men)
Grenadier Company of Agenois (73 men)
Chasseur Company of Gatinois (80 men)
Right Column: Count Arthur Dillon
Volunteer Grenadier Company, Captain Moedermotte (60 men)
Fusilier Company of Dillon (256 men)
Grenadier Company of Auxerrois (57 men)
Grenadier Company of Foix (83 men)
Grenadier Company of Dillon (94 men)
Grenadier Company of Guadeloupe (50 men)
Chasseur Company of Guadeloupe (51 men)
Grenadier Company of Cambresis (88 men)
Grenadier Company of Haynault (85 men)
Chasseur Company of Champagne (67 men)
Chasseur Company of Le Cap (50 men)
Chasseur Company of Port au Prince (47 men)
Dismounted Dragoons of Conde and of Belzunce detachment (30 men)
Left Column: Baron de Steding
Regiment of Fusiliers
 Fusilier Company of Armagnac (175 men)
 Fusilier Company of Auxerrois (134 men)
 Fusilier Company of Foix (203 men)
 Fusilier Company of Walsh (26 men)
 Fusilier Company of Cambresis (94 men)
 Fusilier Company of Haynault (208 men)
 Fusilier Company of Le Cap (47 men)
 Fusilier Company of Guadeloupe (135 men)
 Fusilier Company of Port au Prince (87 men)
Dismounted Dragoons of Conde and of Belzunce detachment (23 men)
Reserve Column: General Le Vicomte Louis Marie de Noailles
Reserve force composed of men from various regiments in assault column (400 men)
2 x 6lb cannons (60 men)
Troops remaining entrenched: Major-General Jean-Claude-Louis de Sablières
Volunteer Chasseurs (mulattos) of San Domingo (540 men)
Volunteer Grenadiers (mulattos) of San Domingo, Major des Français (66 men)
Royal Corps of Marines (337 men)
Chasseur Company of Martinique (52 men)
Fusilier Company of Martinique (36 men)
Dragoons of Conde and of Belzunce detachment (20 men)
Artillery batteries
Right Battery
Royal Corps of Marines (108 men)
5 x 18lb cannons
11 x 12lb cannons
Left Battery
Gunners (100 men)
Volunteer Chasseurs of San Domingo (40 men)
6 x 18lb cannons
6 x 12lb cannons
Mortar Battery
Bombardiers of the Navy (30 men)
Volunteer Chasseurs of San Domingo (30 men)
9 x 9in. mortars
French Total: 4,567 men and 28 cannons and 9 mortars
Allied Total: 7,722 men and 38 cannons and 9 mortars

BRITISH FORCES: MAJOR-GENERAL AUGUSTINE PREVOST

71st Regiment, Lieutenant-Colonel John Maitland
 1st Battalion, Major Archibald McArthur (282 men)
 2nd Battalion, Major McDonald (407 men)
 Light Dragoons, Captain Thomas Tawes (47 men)
Light Corps, Major Colin Graham
 16th Regiment (11 men)
 Light Infantry companies from 16th, 60th, 71st Regiments (331 men)
60th Regiment
 2nd Battalion (50 men)
 3rd Battalion (65 men)
 4th Battalion (116 men)
Hessian Grenadier Regiment von Trumbach (293 men)
Hessian Garrison Regiment von Wissenbach, Lieutenant-Colonel Friedrich von Porbeck (529 men)
Royal Marines (40 men)
New York Volunteers, Major Sheridan (220 men)
DeLancy's Loyalist Regiment
 1st Battalion, Lieutenant-Colonel John Cruger (148 men)
 2nd Battalion
New Jersey Volunteers, 3rd Battalion, Lieutenant-Colonel Allen (302 men)
East Florida Rangers, Lieutenant-Colonel Thomas Brown (178 men)
South Carolina Royalists, Colonel Alexander Innes
 1st Battalion (276 men)
 2nd Battalion (109 men)
North Carolina Volunteers, Lieutenant-Colonel John Hamilton (126 men)
Georgia Loyalist and Volunteers, Major Wright (111 men)
City of Savannah Loyal Militia (200 men)
Black Pioneers (277 men)
Sailors (117 men)
Royal Artillery (109 men)
 2 x 18lb cannons
 2 x 12lb cannons
 72 x (6lb and 9lb) cannons
 8 x (3lb and 4lb) cannons
Royal Navy
 HMS *Germaine*
 HMS *Fowey*
 Armed Brig *Keppel*
British Total: 4,813 men and 84 cannons

OPPOSING PLANS

AMERICAN PLANS

As the Revolutionary flames spread throughout the colonies, they did not take hold in Georgia until January 1776 when the Royal Governor James Wright was placed under house arrest. He was allowed to take his seat as the governor, but served only as a figurehead to the newly established Patriot (Whig) Council of Safety to govern Savannah and Georgia. The following month several British ships arrived, unaware of the change in government, although the Patriots believed the ships were sent to support Wright. In the confusion, he was able to escape. Shortly thereafter, several other British ships arrived to procure rice and provisions for the British troops besieged in Boston, although Wright and the British captains tried to negotiate with the Council to procure the supplies that were on vessels sitting at anchor outside of Savannah but to no avail. In early March, the British forced the issue, and in what became the Battle of the Rice Boats, captured the vessels and sailed them to Boston.

Another concern for the Council of Safety was the constant threat of Native American incursion in the back-country. They realized the best way to neutralize the Cherokee and Creek Native American threat in the Georgia and Carolina back-country was to maintain an active militia force. Furthermore, the presence of a British Army and Tory threats from the south gave immediate attention to leaders to take control of British East Florida. As the Rebellion spread into all counties of Georgia and South Carolina, hundreds of Loyalists were forced from their homes by their Whig neighbors and fled south to Florida creating food shortages in that state, that initiated raids into southern Georgia's rich agricultural areas.

On three separate occasions between 1776 and 1778, colonial Continental and militia forces unsuccessfully attempted to

Brigadier-General Lachlan McIntosh, Continental officer and leader of the second expedition to capture East Florida. He killed Button Gwinnett in a duel and as a result was transferred to the Northern Department. He eventually returned to the Southern Department and led a brigade of South Carolina Continental troops during the siege and attack on Savannah. (Library of Congress)

The situation in the South, December 1775 to October 1778

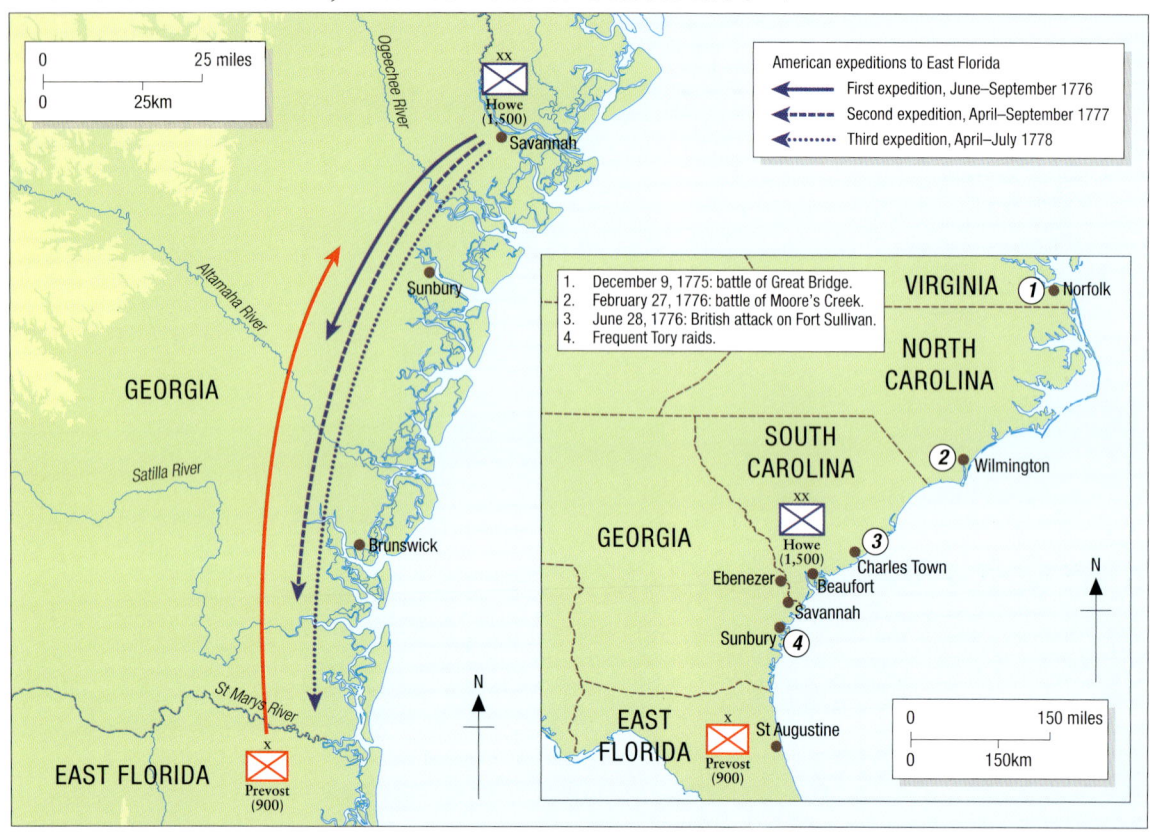

Button Gwinnett, president of the Georgia Council of Safety and commander-in-chief of the Georgia militia during the second expedition against East Florida. He was a signatory to the Declaration of Independence. (Georgia Historical Society)

capture British-held East Florida and St Augustine. The first attempt in 1776 was led by General Charles Lee who had organized a small force of Georgians, Carolinians, and Virginians but was turned away not by the British but by yellow fever and malaria in the steamy swamps along the Ogeechee River. In September 1776, while at Sunbury, Georgia General Lee was recalled by the Continental Congress to the northern theater and took with him the North Carolina and Virginia troops. Brigadier-General Robert Howe with General Lee at Sunbury was given command of the Southern Department and eventually called off the expedition. That same year, the South Carolina militia aggressively pursued and defeated the Cherokees in western South Carolina, reducing the threat to settlers in the back-country for a period of time. The fear of Native American raids and potential gatherings of Loyalists in the back-country would remain a constant fear for Patriots in these two states. Moreover, Patriots feared and distrusted neighbors who would not take an oath against the king, which often led them to force those families from their homes. The continuous conflict between former neighbors heightened the retaliatory responses in Georgia by Loyalist ranger groups operating from East Florida.

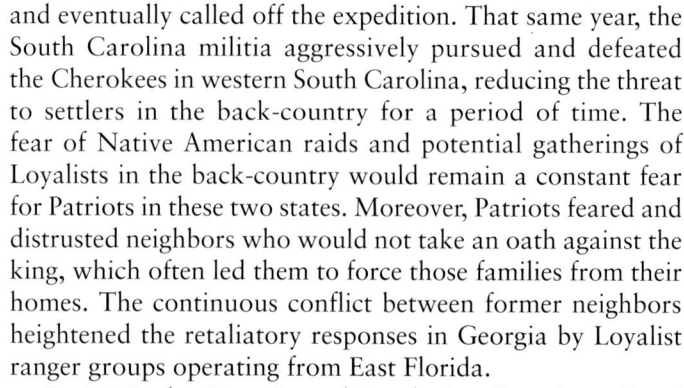

In 1777, the Georgia and South Carolina Councils of Safety urged another drive against St Augustine. Although this expedition neared the Georgia–Florida border at New

Brunswick, it too was aborted because of constant bickering between the two senior commanders about who was in overall charge of the expedition and the lack of logistical support. The two commanders, Brigadier-General Lachlan McIntosh, a Continental officer who firmly believed he was in charge, as compared to Button Gwinnett, President of the Georgia Council of Safety and commander-in-chief of the Georgia's militia, who believed he did not have to take orders from McIntosh. Even though Gwinnett had no military authority, he began to quarrel with McIntosh, even before the expedition departed Savannah. In May 1777, their disagreement eventually led to a duel and, as a result of his wound, Gwinnett died several days later. Under intense pressure from the Georgia assembly, the Continental Congress transferred McIntosh to Washington's northern army.

The third and final attempt to capture St Augustine was in 1778, led by Brigadier-General Howe but it too ended near the St Marys River on June 28. Howe experienced, first hand, the difficulty as a Continental officer of leading state militia formations which firmly believed that they reported to their state leaders and not to a Continental officer. In this expedition, Howe had direct control of the Continental troops whereas Georgia Governor John Houstoun commanded the Georgia militia and General Andrew Williamson led the South Carolina militia. The animosity surfaced when Houstoun, the 27-year-old lawyer and newly selected Governor, rebelled against Howe's

Christopher Gadsden, a popular political figure in the South Carolina assembly in Charles Town, openly criticized General Howe's lack of leadership and character in the third failed expedition to East Florida. His public and written discourse came to a head on August 30, 1778 when Howe challenged Gadsden to a duel. (Library of Congress)

The Gadsden Flag, designed by Christopher Gadsden in February 1776, presented the provincial congress with the coiled rattlesnake and motto "Don't Tread On Me" on a yellow background. (National Archives)

authority and insisted that neither he nor his militia had to follow orders from the Southern Department commander. By mid-July the expedition had only some 350 men fit for service, so Howe ordered a withdrawal, never having come close to their objective. He would later write of this expedition, "If I am ever again to depend upon operations I have no right to guide and men I have no right to command, I shall deem it then, as now I do, one of the most unfortunate accidents of my life." Although the Georgia and South Carolina leadership let General Howe down, it saw the failure as a result of Howe's incompetence rather than its shortcomings. One public critic was Christopher Gadsden, a former brigadier-general in the Continental service and popular political figure in the South Carolina assembly in Charles Town, who openly criticized Howe's lack of leadership and moral character. It was widely known that Howe enjoyed the company of women. Some felt Gadsden's fury was only personal since he had been passed over for the Southern Department command by the Continental Congress appointment of General Robert Howe and soon after had resigned his commission. This public and written discourse came to a head on August 30, when Howe challenged Gadsden to a duel. The duel ended with Gadsden receiving a minor wound to his ear; in reply Gadsden fired his pistol in the air as a sign of his apology to Howe, and they would become lifelong friends. By September 1778, the Continental Congress, in response to the mounting criticism from the Georgia and South Carolina Assemblies against Howe's performance, selected Major-General Benjamin Lincoln to replace Howe.

D'Estaing disembarked a large French force of several hundred troops aided by hundreds of local inhabitants and convinced the British to surrender St Vincent on June 18, 1779. (Library of Congress)

FRENCH PLANS

Comte d'Estaing's fleet, consisting of 12 ships of the line and five frigates along with transports that carried 4,000 troops, departed Toulon, France on April 13, 1778. In three months, d'Estaing arrived off the Delaware Bay coast in July as per his original orders, but arrived too late to interfere with the British withdrawal from Philadelphia. He then sailed north to New York and arrived off Sandy Hook (New Jersey) while Admiral Richard Howe's British fleet was anchored in New York City Bay. General Washington quickly dispatched Colonels Laurens and Hamilton to meet with d'Estaing and brief him on the current situation and to get pilots for his vessels to guide them across the Sandy Hook sandbar. They informed d'Estaing that the alternate course of action was to attack the British garrison at Newport, Rhode Island.

The pilots acquired, unanimously declared they could not navigate the deep draft ships of d'Estaing's fleet without risk of running aground near the sand barrier. D'Estaing informed Washington that he would sail for Newport. In conjunction with this move, Washington authorized General John Sullivan to call out 5,000 militia and with the support of

The voyage of the Comte d'Estaing

1. April 1778: d'Estaing departs Toulon, France.
2. July 1778: arrives off the Delaware Coast.
3. August 1778: naval battle off Rhode Island coast.
4. September 1778: repairs in Boston, Massachusetts.
5. December 1778: inconclusive battle off St Lucia.
6. June 19, 1779: capture of the Island of St Vincent.
7. July 4, 1779: capture of the Island of Grenada.
8. September–October 1779: siege of Savannah, Georgia.
9. October 1779: d'Estaing returns to France.

D'Estaing's force assaulted the British defenses on Grenada, forcing their surrender on July 4, 1779. (Library of Congress)

Lafayette's two Continental brigades joined forces with d'Estaing's troops for a combined attack. The fleet arrived off Newport on July 29, where Sullivan met with d'Estaing on his flagship and agreed on a joint attack set for August 10. The next day, while the French were at anchorage within the Narraganset Bay, reports came in announcing the approach of Howe's fleet from New York. Despite protests from Sullivan, d'Estaing ordered his troops to re-embark their ships. On August 10, d'Estaing's fleet got under way to meet the British fleet. For the next 24 hours the two fleets maneuvered to gain an advantageous wind position to engage but were met by a severe storm of hurricane-strength winds that dispersed both fleets. As the weather cleared, d'Estaing returned to Newport and met with the American commanders on

British Admiral Byron engaged d'Estaing's fleet on July 6, 1779. Although severely outnumbered, Byron's fleet was able to withdraw following d'Estaing's hesitation and lack of pursuit. D'Estaing's commanders renewed their concerns about his leadership abilities. (Drawing by Bernard Harris)

30

his flagship to inform them he could no longer support an attack and would sail to Boston for repairs, since Howe's fleet returned to New York City. As the French fleet departed, General Sullivan publicly shared his frustration with d'Estaing.

Following the needed repairs, d'Estaing set sail to the Caribbean. His pursuant operations in the Caribbean during the summer of 1779 resulted in the capture of St Vincent and Grenada. He failed to recapture St Lucia, which had recently been reinforced by Major-General James Grant and 5,000 British troops sent by General Clinton the previous year.

By the summer of 1779, a ship arrived from Charles Town with a number of requests for d'Estaing to help clear Georgia of the British. Although d'Estaing had received orders for him and a number of his ships to return to France and, despite the approaching hurricane season, he desperately wanted to strike at least one successful operation in America against the British. By September 4, 1779, his ships were reported off the Georgia coast.

BRITISH PLANS

The southern colonies were never far from the minds of British military planners. Unfortunately, the British losses in 1775 at Great Bridge, Virginia and in 1776 at Moore's Creek, North Carolina forced the British to reevaluate their early plans for the southern colonies. In February 1776 a large population of Scottish Highlanders living in the back-country of North Carolina had formed a group and marched toward the coast to support the Royal Governor, Josiah Martin. The Highlanders pursued a Patriot group for several days until they set up a defensive position at a bridge over Moore's Creek near Wilmington. On February 27, a young and impulsive Captain Donald McLeod led his Highlanders across the bridge. As they charged with their broadswords and muskets, they yelled "King George and Broadsword" but were cut down within 15 minutes. Their defeat erased any hopes the British had of securing North Carolina early into the rebellion. The Loyalist losses at Moore's Creek made General Henry Clinton, leading a force to establish a base at Wilmington, reconsider his plans, since he would not have any Loyalist support in the city or surrounding countryside. Within the next three months, Clinton decided to strike at the South Carolina capital. He led a naval and ground attack to capture the fort and garrison on Sullivan Island, guarding the entrance to Charles Town. Clinton's unsuccessful attack in June 1776 buoyed the revolutionary fervor in the Deep South. In addition, the colonial militia was able to defeat the Cherokee Nation in 1776, minimizing the Tory influence over the Native Americans and keep them from rampaging over their western boundaries. Although the defeat was a temporary setback, John Stuart, Superintendent of Indian Affairs, maintained vigorous trade negotiations directly and through his representatives to keep favor with the Cherokee, Creek, and Seminole tribes to support the British cause.

The Charles Town home of John Stuart's family. As Royal Superintendent of Indian Affairs for the southern district from Virginia to Florida, Stuart had to leave the city, but his family remained at their home. From his headquarters in Pensacola, Florida, he was instrumental in gaining the trust and confidence of the Cherokee Nation, Seminoles and other tribes in the district who referred to him as their "Beloved Father." Upon his death on March 21, 1779, General Clinton wrote to Lord Germain: "The loss of so faithful and useful a servant to His Majesty is at all times to be regretted, but at this critical juncture is most sincerely to be lamented." (Library of Congress)

The decision to launch an attack with British regulars against the southern colonies in 1778 was based on two premises. First, British naval supremacy could transport an overwhelming force against a particular objective and give the British the initiative against the American forces. The entry of the French into the war would speed up the British timetable, but hopefully they would arrive too late to stop an overwhelming British victory. The second premise was the enthusiasm of the loyal subjects in Georgia and the Carolinas as advocated by the former Royal Governors and wealthy landowners of those states. The true lack of enthusiasm southern Loyalists had for the British would be felt in 1779. Although a number of the populace were loyal, the string of defeats in previous years and the intimidation by many rebel groups left many disheartened and reluctant Loyalists, who were disinclined to support the British fully. Furthermore, those loyal southern subjects who did not flee to East Florida, were apprehensive about openly taking up arms against their neighbors because of the lack of protection from the British regulars and reprisals by Patriot militia.

East Florida Royal Governor Patrick Tonyn constantly disagreed with Augustine Prevost over issues until Prevost's promotion to general. The two contentious issues were Tonyn's aggressive intentions to reclaim Georgia, compared with Prevost's defensive mindset to only protect East Florida and the direct control of the East Florida Loyalist Rangers. (Anne S.K. Brown Military Collection)

THE CAMPAIGN

The period from December 1778 through October 1779, marked the renewed efforts of the British, led by Lord George Germain, Secretary of State for the American Department, to adopt a southern strategy to bring an eventual end to the Revolution. The first phase of this campaign was the capture of Savannah, Georgia. General Sir Henry Clinton, commander of the British force in America, selected Lieutenant-Colonel Archibald Campbell to lead an expedition of 3,000 troops to Georgia. On November 8, 1778 Campbell received Clinton's orders which read: "Sir, You will be pleased to proceed with the Troops embarked under your Command, and by rapid Movement endeavor to take possession of Savannah in the Province of Georgia." The instructions further stated, "It being the Intention of the Command in Chief to dispatch you upon a Service, the Result of which, if successful, may possibly open the Way for the Re-establishment of Civil Government with the Provinces of Georgia and South Carolina."

The next day Campbell and Commodore Hyde Parker, the fleet commander for the expedition, embarked on Parker's 44-gun flagship HMS *Phoenix*. Captain Parker was given the rank of Commodore of the expedition by the newly appointed Rear Admiral Gambier, who had recently replaced Admiral Howe, as the British fleet commander in North America. Onboard, Campbell summarized Clinton's instruction, that he could accomplish conquering the provinces of Georgia and South Carolina but with twice as many troops, assuming 6,000 Loyalists would rally to the King's colors from the back-countries and from Native American support.

Campbell's force sailed from Staten Island, on November 12 but had to anchor near Sandy Hook for 16 days because of adverse weather conditions and had to wait for an adequate replacement transport ship for the artillery and stores, since the original ship was damaged in the storm. The British had learned that not all merchants placed under contract were reliable; there were a number of instances of the ship's master sailing into a Patriot city and selling the British supplies. The fleet eventually sailed on November 26, although the secrecy about the purpose of the expedition had been exposed, Campbell wrote in his journal: "whole fleet sailed from the Hook, the troops in high Health and Spirits, and the Wind favorable and moderate." The expedition was composed of both battalions from the 71st Regiment of Highlanders (less the grenadier companies), two Hessian regiments, and Loyalists from New York and New Jersey. Clinton's initial plan was for Campbell to seize Savannah and for General Prevost to move to the Altamaha River near New Brunswick and support Campbell if required.

The situation in the South, November–December 1778

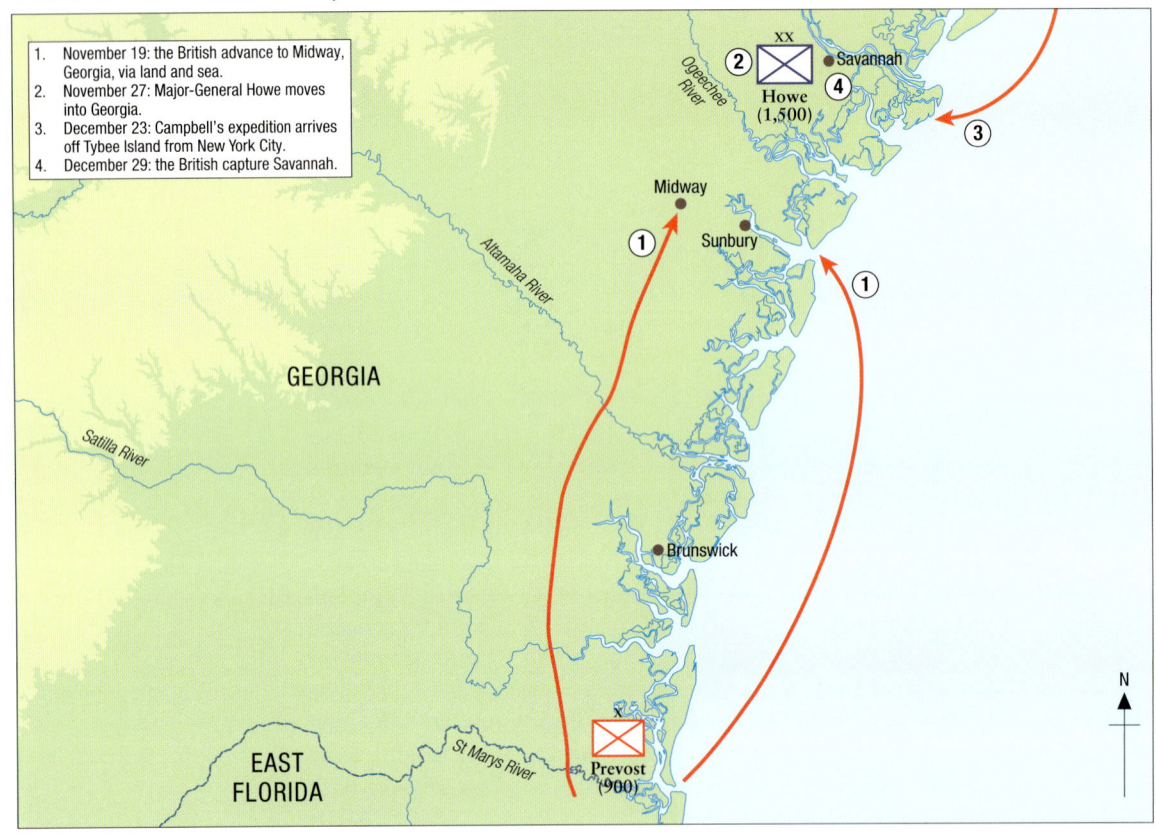

1. November 19: the British advance to Midway, Georgia, via land and sea.
2. November 27: Major-General Howe moves into Georgia.
3. December 23: Campbell's expedition arrives off Tybee Island from New York City.
4. December 29: the British capture Savannah.

MIDWAY

Meanwhile, in St Augustine, because of mounting pressure to provision the increasing numbers of Loyalist families moving into East Florida, which prior to the war had a population of 3,000 people, General Prevost on November 11, 1778 dispatched a ground and amphibious force to Sunbury, Georgia. Its purpose was to gather cattle, provisions and if feasible capture the fort protecting Sunbury, since it had been used as a staging base for the failed Patriot attempts to invade East Florida. The ground force led by Lieutenant-Colonel James Marcus Prevost, consisting of 100 British regulars, 300 rangers and Native Americans, marched from St Augustine and entered Georgia near New Brunswick on November 19, 1778. Although Lieutenant-Colonel Prevost's force engaged in sporadic skirmishes with Georgia militia, it reached Midway, Georgia on November 24. Colonel John White, commanding the Continental troops stationed at Sunbury, had led his force and various detachments of Georgia militia totaling over 100 men to meet Prevost near Midway. He ordered Lieutenant-Colonel John McIntosh with about 100 men to stay behind to defend Sunbury and its fort. At Midway, White was joined by Brigadier-General James Screven and 20 of his Georgia militiamen. The two commanders agreed they were not strong enough to defend their current position successfully, and decided to set up an ambush about 1.5 miles south of their position. In a twist of fate Prevost and White had the same idea about an ambush and in a brief skirmish Screven fell, mortally wounded. Prevost believed he was outnumbered because his men had intercepted a dispatch to that effect, which was in fact a ruse White used to mislead him, and ordered a withdrawal. In addition, Prevost had received no word from the amphibious force and believed he had accomplished his mission. His force, which had collected over 2,000 head of cattle, a large number of horses, provisions, and about 200 freed slaves, headed back to St Augustine. Before returning, they burned down the Midway Meeting House, which was a known assembly point for rebel militia.

SUNBURY

The amphibious incursion led by Lieutenant-Colonel Lewis Fuser arrived at the Medway River on November 24, having encountered strong headwinds on its transit from St Augustine. Fuser disembarked his 500-man force and marched to Sunbury. Upon entering the town, they found only a loyalist family and a physician under parole with his family; the remaining residents had evacuated to the fort on the outskirts of town, sitting on a low bluff overlooking the Medway River. On November 25, Fuser's men were in position along with their light cannons and he felt confident to demand the fort's surrender. Fuser wrote to McIntosh, the 23-year-old in charge of the fort, "The resistance you can, or intend to make, will only bring destruction upon this country. On the contrary, if you will deliver me the fort which you command, and lay down your arms and remain neutral until the fate of America is determined, you shall, as well as all the inhabitants of this parish, remain in peaceable possession of your property." He expected a response within the hour. The Scottish-born and defiant McIntosh replied, "We would rather perish in a vigorous defense than accept your proposals. We, Sir, are fighting the battles of America, and therefore, disdain to remain neutral till its fate is determined. As to surrendering the fort, receive this laconic reply: Come and take it." Fuser, surprised by the defiant tone of McIntosh's reply and upon hearing of Prevost's withdrawal, declined to attack the fort and withdrew his force back along the inland waterways to St Augustine. The garrison, in celebration of their achievement, named it Fort Morris to honor its commander of Artillery, Captain Thomas Morris. Furthermore, for his audacious response to Fuser, the Georgia legislature eventually awarded McIntosh a sword with the words "Come and Take It" engraved on it.

Upon hearing news of his replacement as the Southern Department Commander by Major-General Benjamin Lincoln and of the British incursion into Georgia, General Howe at his headquarters in Charles Town wrote to the President of Congress that he was marching into Georgia to counter the British advance from St Augustine. Howe's force consisted of 1,000 men from the 1st and 2nd Georgia and 3rd, 4th and 5th South Carolina Continentals along with various South Carolina militia units. On November 27, his force reached the Zubley Ferry, on the Savannah River, some 30 miles from Savannah and crossed into Georgia. As Howe's force continued to move south, he learned of the Midway skirmish and of Fuser's abortive attempt to capture the Sunbury fort. Howe then decided to send detachments from his force to various strategic points along the Georgian coast to sound the alarm in the event of any British naval presence and especially of any troop debarkations. Furthermore, on December 6, Howe had learned of Campbell's expedition and rumor that his objective was Savannah. Two days later while at Sunbury, Howe wrote to obtain help from Georgia Governor Houstoun and militia to prepare the defenses of Savannah and Sunbury to counter Campbell's pending expedition, but to no avail. Although the Continental Congress did pass resolutions requesting Virginia and North Carolina to send 1,000 and 3,000 soldiers respectively to support the Southern Department, the Georgia and South Carolina governors and officials decided on their own to ignore Howe and correspond directly with General Lincoln who had arrived in Charles Town on December 7 to assume duties as the Southern Department commander.

CAPTURE OF SAVANNAH

During Campbell's transit to Savannah, Commodore Parker dispatched HMS *Granby* on December 5 to St Augustine, with Campbell's letters to East Florida Governor Tonyn and General Prevost, who received their respective letters on December 19. The proclamation would set the conditions in Georgia for the return of Royal Governor Wright. The contents of the letter to Governor Tonyn read:

> By the latest intelligence from the back Countries, there is Reason to believe a considerable Body of Loyalists are happily disposed to join the Royal Standard: To encourage that laudable Spirit, and favour their Junction, I mean as soon as proper post shall be established at the Town of Savannah, to move with the Army as far up the Country as the Strength and Disposition of the Enemy will admit ... I have the Honour to enclose a Copy of the Proclamation which I mean to issue upon Landing.

In addition, the same contents of the letter were received by General Prevost, but with the additional request: "in which Case I would beg Leave to suggest, that it might be of Importance, the Superintendent of Indian Affairs [Captain John Stuart] would make a Diversion in my favour along the Back Woods of Georgia even as far as the Frontiers of South Carolina." Stuart in Pensacola did not receive the direction from General Prevost to support Campbell's request until early March 1779.

On December 23, 1778, Campbell's force, less one transport carrying New Jersey Loyalists which became separated during the transit from New York, disembarked at Tybee Island at the mouth of the Savannah River, some 16 miles from Savannah. Not having any maps of the area, on December 25, Campbell sent an expedition under the command of Captain Sir James Baird to gather intelligence about the defenses of Savannah. Baird returned the following morning with an overseer and slave named Peter who indicated Howe's strength and disposition of his forces in Savannah.

Today's view, as seen from the point of view of the British approach to Brewton's Bluff. Lieutenant-Colonel Campbell noted, "Had the rebels stationed four Pieces of Cannon on the Bluff ... it is more than probable, they would have destroyed the greatest part of this Division of our little Army in their progress to the Bluff." (Photograph by Scott Martin)

Meanwhile, Howe held a council of war with his commanders to decide if they should defend Savannah or withdraw into South Carolina and wait for General Lincoln. To complicate his situation, many local merchants urged him to defend the city. For the next two days, having to contend with unfavorable winds and the tide on the Savannah River, Parker's ships were not able to cross the sandbar until the afternoon of December 28. As the ships proceeded up the river, lookouts spotted three enemy galleys near the city. Keeping at a distance, Campbell assessed that the only landing place for his troops was near the Girardeau Plantation, about one mile due east of Savannah. As evening set, Campbell had assembled his landing party of light infantry on flat boats to begin its debarkation at first light.

On the morning of December 29, the light infantry company under Captain Cameron landed first, followed by the first division under the command of Lieutenant-Colonel John Maitland, consisting of the 1st Battalion 71st Regiment and 1st Battalion of DeLancey's Brigade along with two small cannons. The forces quickly moved inland along the causeway (road), which was about 600 yards at a right angle to the river and ran directly toward the Girardeau Plantation on Brewton's Bluff. On either side of the causeway was a rice swamp and bordered by a deep ditch on either side, which gradually ascended to Brewton's 40ft bluff. Howe had sent Captain Smith and 50 men to occupy the plantation and bluff area. Smith, unsure of his commander's intent, had his men prepare a suitable defensive position by removing planks from the sides of the buildings to enable them to fire from a concealed position. Smith knew how narrow the causeway was and felt confident his men could hold for a period of time if he was attacked from that direction. Upon their landing, Lieutenant-Colonel Maitland leading the initial force and Campbell, who came ashore with the 71st, agreed they would have to rush any troops defending the bluffs at the end of the causeway, since it was wide enough for only two men. Campbell ordered a small force to serve as a forlorn hope to be the first ones in to attack. The initial charge would be made by Captain Cameron and four Highlanders, followed immediately by a sergeant and 12 men and about 50 yards behind them would be 500 troops all in a column of two men. Smith's men allowed the forlorn party and supporting party to come within 100 yards of the buildings and opened fire. Captain Cameron and three of his light infantrymen were killed in the three-minute engagement. Campbell, who accompanied the main body, noted afterwards, "the rebels retreated with precipitation by the Back Doors and Windows."

In preparation for a British landing and attack, Howe held another council of war with his commanders that morning to select the ground to make their stand. Just a few days earlier, Governor Houstoun finally authorized the Georgia militia to fall under Howe's command. About a half-mile southeast of the city, Howe established his line of defense. He formed a line in the shape of a semicircle, with the ends anchored by swampy rice fields and old

Today's view as seen from Lieutenant-Colonel Campbell's left flank along the causeway to Brewton's Bluff. (Photograph by Scott Martin)

BRITISH UNITS
A. 1/71st Regiment, Woellwarth Regiment and 71st Light Infantry
B. 1/71st Forlorn Party
C. 1/71st Regiment and Woellwarth Hessian Regiment
D. 71st Light Infantry, NY Loyalists

CAMPBELL

GOVERNOR WRIGHT'S PLANTATION

GIRARDEAU'S PLANTATION

BREWTON'S BLUFF

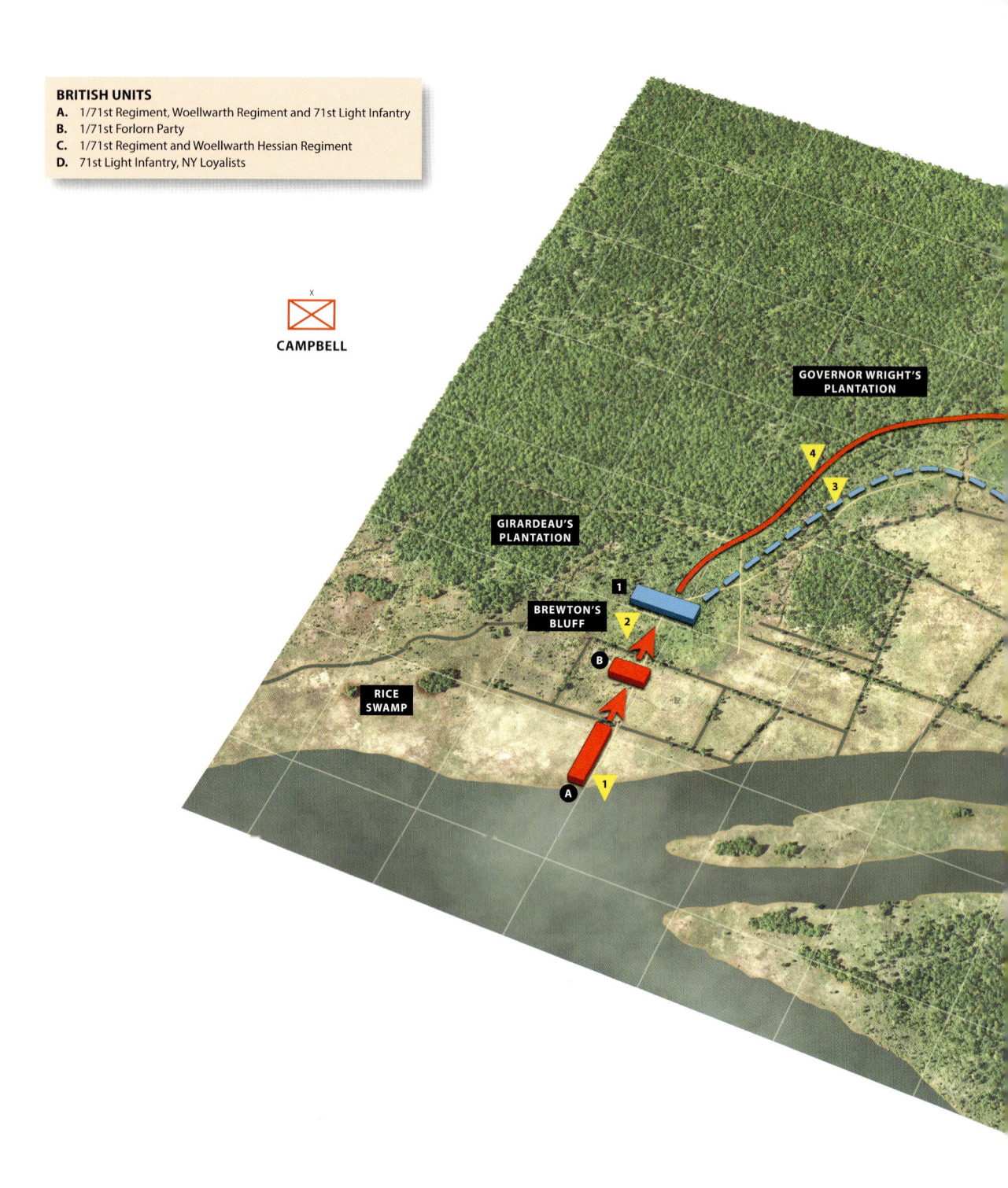

RICE SWAMP

EVENTS

1. The British land by boat.
2. A brief fight at Brewton's Bluff.
3. Captain Smith and his 50 men retreat.
4. The British advance to Governor Wright's plantation.
5. The British form up on high ground south-east of Savannah.
6. The British Light Infantry moves around to attack the American right flank.
7. The British Light Infantry attacks.
8. The British launch simultaneous attack on American main line.
9. The Georgia and Carolina brigades retreat along with the Georgia Militia.

THE BRITISH CAPTURE SAVANNAH
The first battle for Savannah, December 29, 1778

AMERICAN UNITS
1. Captain Smith's detachment
2. Georgia Brigade
3. South Carolina Brigade
4. Georgia Militia

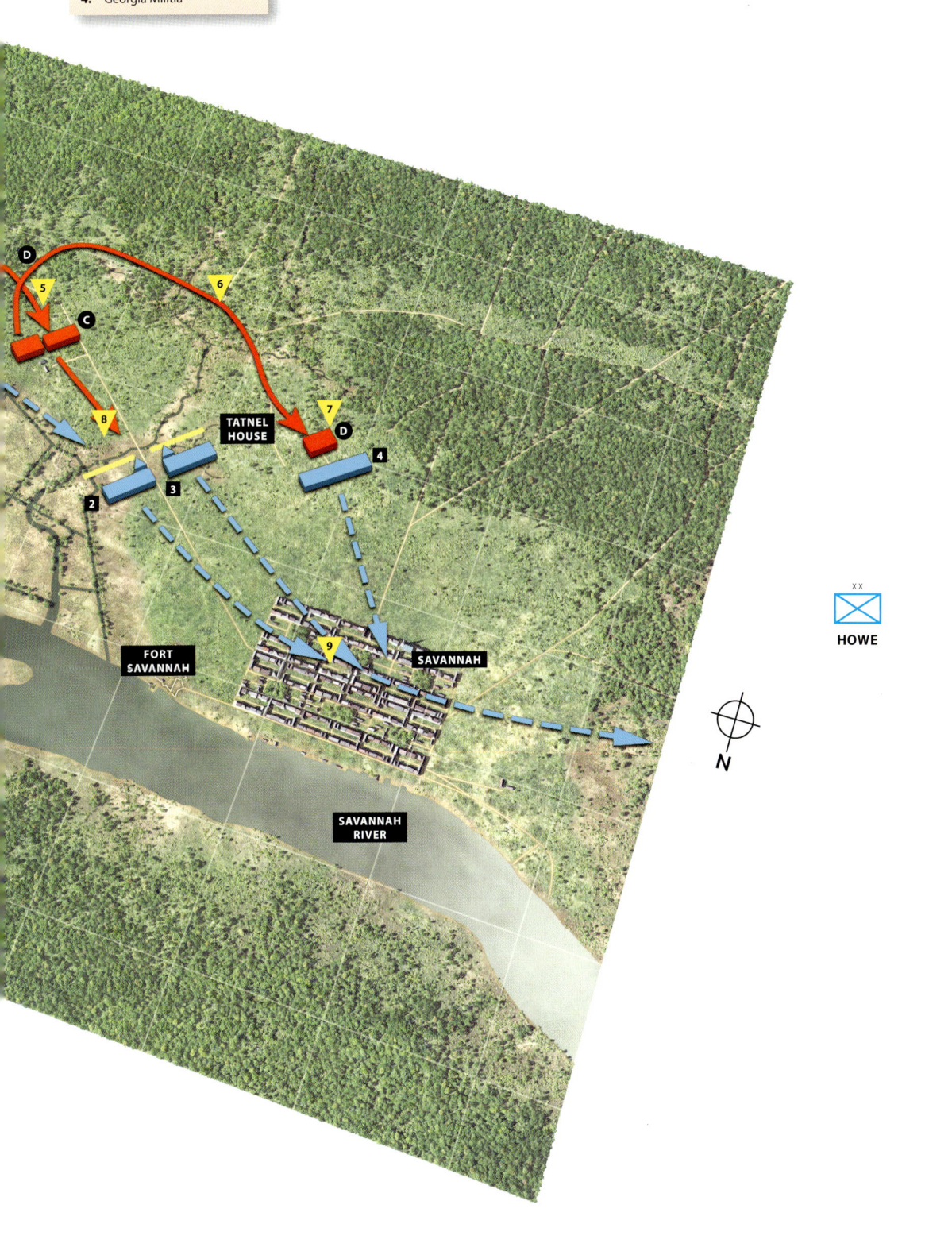

TATNEL HOUSE

FORT SAVANNAH

SAVANNAH

SAVANNAH RIVER

HOWE

N

Today's view of the Fort Morris earthworks. On January 10, 1779, Major Joseph Lane, commanding officer of the garrison, surrendered the fort after a three-day siege and short bombardment. Although Lane had been ordered by General Howe to evacuate Sunbury and the fort, he decided to stay and defend it. Lane erroneously felt he could successfully defend the fort, since he had been second in command of the fort in November, when Lieutenant-Colonel John McIntosh told the British "come and take it." (Photograph by Scott Martin)

Fort Savannah on his left flank, and a wooded swampy area on his right flank. On the left flank, Howe placed the Georgia Continentals and militia under Colonel Samuel Elbert and the South Carolina Continentals under Colonel Isaac Huger and Colonel William Thompson on the right. The line was supported by four pieces of field artillery and his light infantry companies guarded the flanks. Most of Howe's troops, including the Continentals, had seen little to no action in the war and the anticipated action would be against a very disciplined and battle-tested regiment from the northern theater.

As Campbell's light infantry advanced toward Governor Wright's plantation, the rest of his force was disembarking at the landing site. Later in the day, Campbell had assembled his two battalions of the 71st Highland Regiment, two regiments of German soldiers (von Wissenbach and von Woellwarth), and four companies of Loyalists, mostly recruited in New York. When his advance light infantry companies spotted Howe's line, the main body stopped short about 800 yards at one of Governor Wright's plantations giving him a view of the city and of Howe's defensive positions. Campbell climbed a tree on the plantation and used his field glass to examine Howe's positions. He considered Howe's defenses as essentially sound, but a local slave from Wright's plantation named Quamino Dolly told him that there was a path through the wooded and swampy ground on Howe's right flank. Campbell ordered Captain Sir James Baird to take 350 light infantry and about 250 New York Loyalists under the command of Colonel Turnbull and follow the "confidential slave" through the woods and swamp, while he arrayed his troops just out of view in a way that would give the impression of attempting a flanking maneuver on Howe's left near the river. To provide observation to Baird's movement, Major Skelly climbed a tree to observe Baird's progress while still in view from Campbell's position. True to Quamino's word, the trail came out on the main Ogeechee road, near the Continental barracks, guarded by some of Colonel George Walton's Georgia militia; unbeknownst to the Americans they had been outflanked. When Baird reached his attack position, Major Skelly waved his hat to signal all was ready, Campbell then ordered the regulars to charge.

The first sounds of battle Howe heard were from musket fire behind him near the barracks, quickly followed by cannon fire to signal Campbell's main attack. Howe's troops then observed the steady advance of Campbell's Highlanders and Hessian's line of battle towards them from Wright's plantation. Howe, seeing the potential of having his main line trapped between two British forces, ordered an immediate retreat, which rapidly turned into a rout. His untried troops hardly bothered to return fire, some throwing down their weapons before attempting to run away through the city and swampy rice fields west of town. The light infantry in the Continental rear cut off the road to Augusta, the only significant escape route, forcing a mad scramble of retreating troops into the city itself. Soldiers who did not immediately surrender were rumored to have been bayoneted. Huger's South Carolinians, along with Colonel Owen Roberts' cannons, managed to assemble an effective rearguard that enabled the rest of Howe's force to escape. Although some men did manage to escape to the west before the British closed off the city, others were forced to attempt swimming across the swollen Musgrove's Creek just west of Savannah during the Savannah River's high tide, resulting in the death by drowning of 30 men. Campbell gained control of the Georgia capital at a cost of seven killed and 17 wounded. Campbell's force took 453 prisoners, and counted at least 83 dead and 11 wounded from Howe's command. When Howe's 25-mile retreat finally ended at Purysburg, South Carolina he had only 342 men remaining, less than half his original army. He would receive much of the blame for the disaster, as noted by General William Moultrie arguing that he should have either disputed the landing site in force or retreated without battle to keep his army intact. Although General Howe was exonerated in a court martial that inquired into the event, Colonel Henry "Light Horse Harry" Lee noted of the battle: "Never was a victory of such magnitude so completely gained with so little loss."

Immediately following the British entrance into Savannah, alleged scenes of property depredation occurred, contrary to Campbell's orders that stated, "in the most strenuous Terms to the Officers, to shew every Mark of Lenity and Protection to the Inhabitants; and to assure the Troops under their orders that any Act of Violence offered to them in their Persons, Families, or Effects, shall be punished with the most rigid Severity." In his journal, Campbell never mentioned any depredations his men inflicted on the residents of Savannah, however for resident and Patriot Lucy Tondee, her life and that of many other Patriots in Savannah would quickly change. She and others witnessed their tables, chairs and other furniture being thrown onto the streets, along with feather beds ripped apart and strewn with the wind throughout the town. Their residences would eventually be used to quarter British soldiers. In addition, Lucy Tondee had most of her propriety sold by auction by the royal government later in the year, as more British soldiers' wives and families took up residence in Savannah.

Campbell rode through the city and surrounding area the following day and noted in his journal this description of the city: "In short one Side [north] of the Town was secured by the River, the two ends [east, west]

Powder horn used by James Vallotton at Savannah. It is decorated with a variety of wildlife and the words "Don't [tread] on me." (Georgia Historical Society)

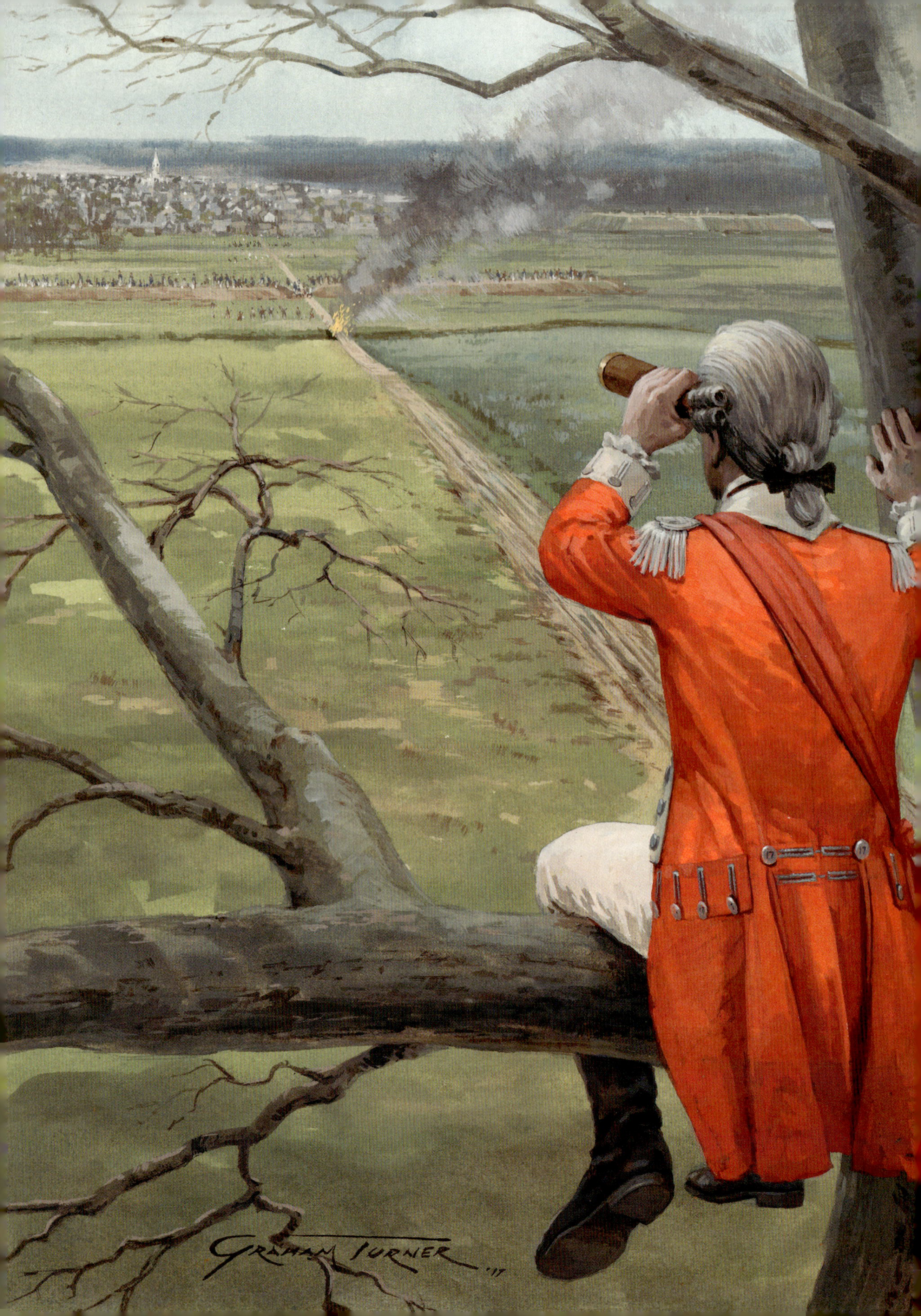
GRAHAM TURNER '17

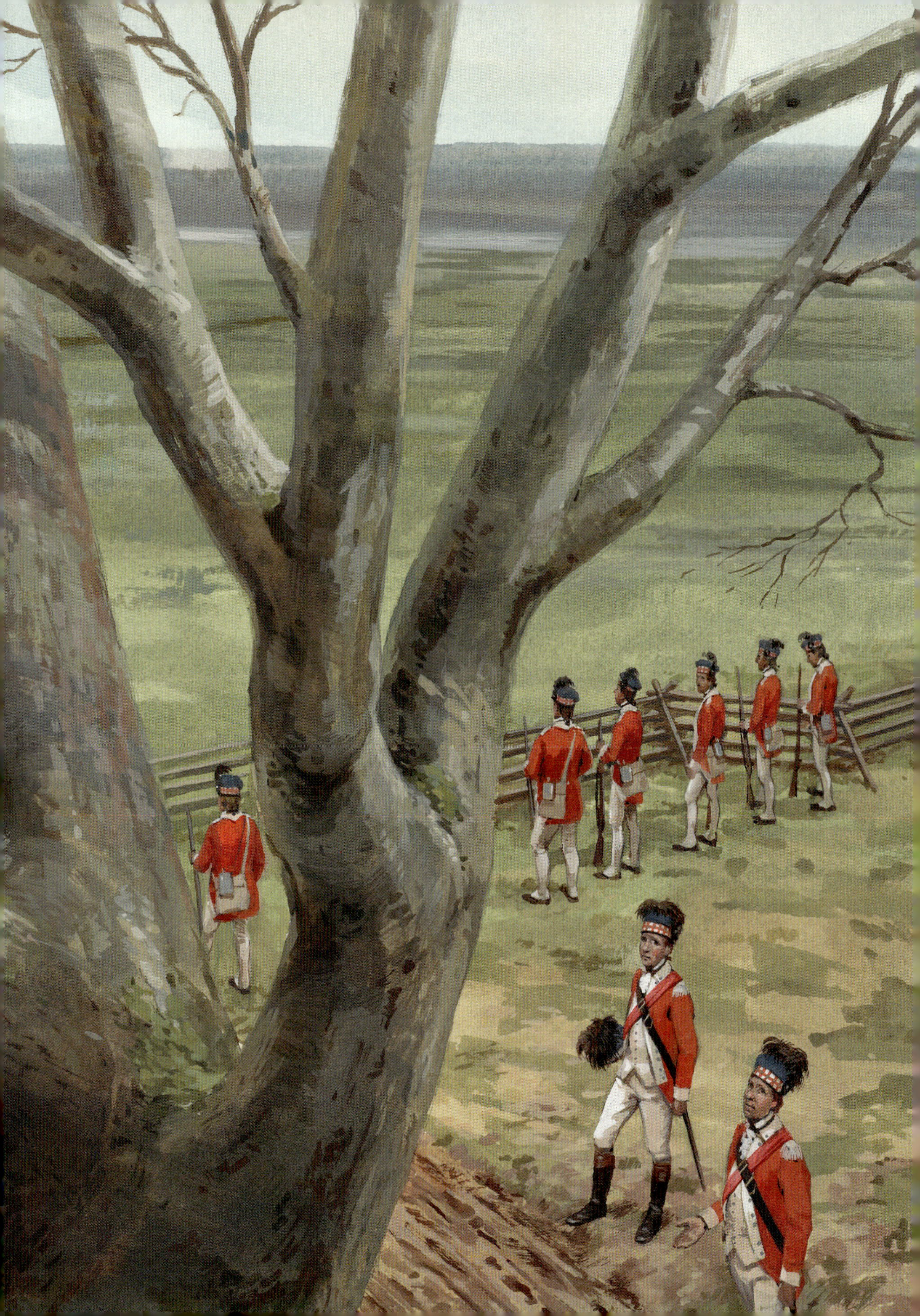

THE CAPTURE OF SAVANNAH, DECEMBER 29, 1778 (PP. 42–43)

Following the British landing on December 29, they advanced under the command of Lieutenant-Colonel Archibald Campbell (1) and by 2pm, the light infantry (2) had reached within 800 yards of the American position and took a position along a rail fence on former Royal Governor Wright's property as the rest of Campbell's column followed behind and remained out of sight from Major-General Howe's force. Campbell climbed a tree of "considerable height" (3) near the road to get a better view of Howe's defensive position. Campbell noted in his journal, "I was enabled to discover that the Rebel Army was formed on a level Piece of Ground, across the Savannah Road, with their Front towards the west, their Right [the South Carolina Brigade under Colonel Isaac Huger] to Tatnel's House joining a thick Woods, which stretched several Miles thence to the Southwards, and their Left [the Georgia Brigade of Continentals and militia under Colonel Samuel Elbert and four cannon in support] was nearly extended to the Rice Swamps on the South east Quarter". Fort Savannah (4) equipped with eight cannon was sited to defend the city from the river approach. Campbell further noted, about 100 yards in front of the Rebel position, was a marshy stream and across it on the Savannah road was a wooden bridge (5). The bridge was on fire and two groups of riflemen were advanced to prevent the British from extinguishing the fire (6).

were shut up by Rice Swamps, and the fourth [south] Side was encircled by an extensive Wood of lofty Pines, the whole very capable of being fortified with advantage." The next day, Campbell departed Savannah with most of his expedition and marched west along the Augusta road following the Savannah River towards Ebenezer to follow slowly Howe's retreating force. He appointed Major MacArthur of the 71st Regiment as the Commandant of Savannah. On January 2, 1779 Campbell's force occupied Ebenezer, 17 miles upstream of Savannah without any resistance. Campbell wrote of Ebenezer as "a small straggling Town on the Bank of the River Savannah, mostly inhabited with Dutch, and situated between two deep Swamps, over which two Wooden Bridges communicate to the Country." The next day, and true to his December 5 letters, Campbell issued the following Proclamation with instructions to be hung on the church door and at every crossroads between Ebenezer and Savannah.

A PROCLAMATION
Whereas the Blessing of peace, Freedom and Protection most graciously tendered by His Majesty to his deluded Subjects of America, have been treated by Congress with repeated Marks of studied Disrespect … BE it therefore known to all His Majesty's Faithful Subjects of the Southern Provinces that a Fleet and Army under Our Orders are actually arrived in Georgia for their protection … uniting their Force under the Royal Standard whereby they may be enabled to rescue their Friends from Oppression, themselves from Slavery … on Condition that they shall immediately return to the Class of peaceable Citizens, acknowledge their first Allegiance to the Crown, and with their Arms support it.

On January 3, as the Proclamations were being hung, across the Savannah River, General Lincoln along with two Continental regiments and North Carolina militia arrived at Purysburg, and united with Howe's men for a combined army of 1,700 men. Lincoln's first impression of Howe's command was an army in total disarray because of its retreat and shaken by its first encounter with the redcoat and Hessian. The small town of Purysburg, first settled by Swiss colonists in 1732 on the Savannah River would become the main position of the southern army to keep watch and vigilance on the British forces across the river. The town was also situated close to the main river ferry and was on the main road between Savannah and Charles Town. Throughout 1779 the Savannah River would serve as a natural boundary between the two armies.

Meanwhile, farther to the south, General Prevost on his own accord crossed into Georgia with 900 men, consisting of the 60th Regiment, several companies from the 16th Regiment, several cannons, South Carolina Loyalists, Brown's East Florida Rangers, and three companies of New Jersey Volunteers, led by Lieutenant-Colonel Isaac Allen, whose transport had been separated from the fleet on their transit from New York. Prevost left about 200 men from the 60th Regiment under the

George Walton, a colonel in the Georgia militia, was wounded and captured at Savannah on December 28, 1778. He was one of the three Georgia delegates to sign off the Declaration of Independence. (State Archives of Florida)

temporary command of Major Beamsley Glazier to garrison St Augustine; he would eventually rejoin Prevost's army later in the year. On January 7, Prevost occupied Sunbury and began a siege of Fort Morris. The siege lasted three days, following a short bombardment and surrender of the garrison by Major Joseph Lane, who had been second in command of the fort in November. The British captured 212 men, with the loss of only one private and three men wounded, whereas the defenders lost three killed and six wounded. Prevost, to honor King George III, changed the fort's name to Fort George.

On January 9, General Lincoln at his headquarters in Purysburg received Campbell's response from Ebenezer regarding the exchange of prisoners, or allowing the officers their paroles. Campbell wrote that the officers could be given their parole and would have to wait until British officers held in the north could be exchanged for them, but with regard to soldiers, he could not give them up unless British soldiers were immediately given for them. Major Thomas Pinckney was Lincoln's negotiator for the initial exchanges with Campbell. Lincoln and Prevost would correspond throughout the year regarding the negotiations for paroles and exchanges of prisoners. The next day, Campbell received a letter from Prevost requesting he send boats and canoes to the Ogeechee River ferry site, 18 miles south of Savannah, to enable his men to cross and march to Savannah.

EXPEDITION TO AUGUSTA

By January 17, British forces consisted of 4,000 men in southern Georgia, along with those in East Florida who fell under the unified command of Brigadier-General Augustine Prevost. As Campbell briefed Prevost on the current situation, Prevost ordered the rank-and-file prisoners captured at Savannah and Fort Morris to be contained in a prison ship at anchor near Savannah and the officers to be sent to Sunbury on their parole until they were exchanged for British officers. Upon Prevost's concurrence, Campbell turned his attention to the Georgia interior for supplies and to foster the support of Loyalists as per Clinton's orders of November 8. On January 20, Campbell wrote to Lord Germain, "I need not inform Your Lordship, how much I prize the hope of being the first British Officer to rend a Stripe and Star from the Flag of Congress." On January 24, Campbell led this expedition (he referred to it as a Corps) to march the 90 miles on the road from Ebenezer to Augusta. His Corps consisted of the following forces:

1st Battalion, 71st Regiment (356 men)
New York Volunteers (175 men)
Sir James Baird's Light Infantry (299 men)
One troop of Light Dragoons (42 men)
Brown's Florida Rangers (72 men)
South Carolina Loyalists (75 men)
2 x 6lb and 2 x 3lb cannons, and 1 x 5.5in. howitzer (25 men)

The two Hessian battalions (903 men) and DeLancy's 2nd Battalion would initially remain in Savannah while the 2nd Battalion of the 71st would remain near Ebenezer and Zubley's Ferry, 23 miles west of Savannah along the river.

The expedition to Augusta

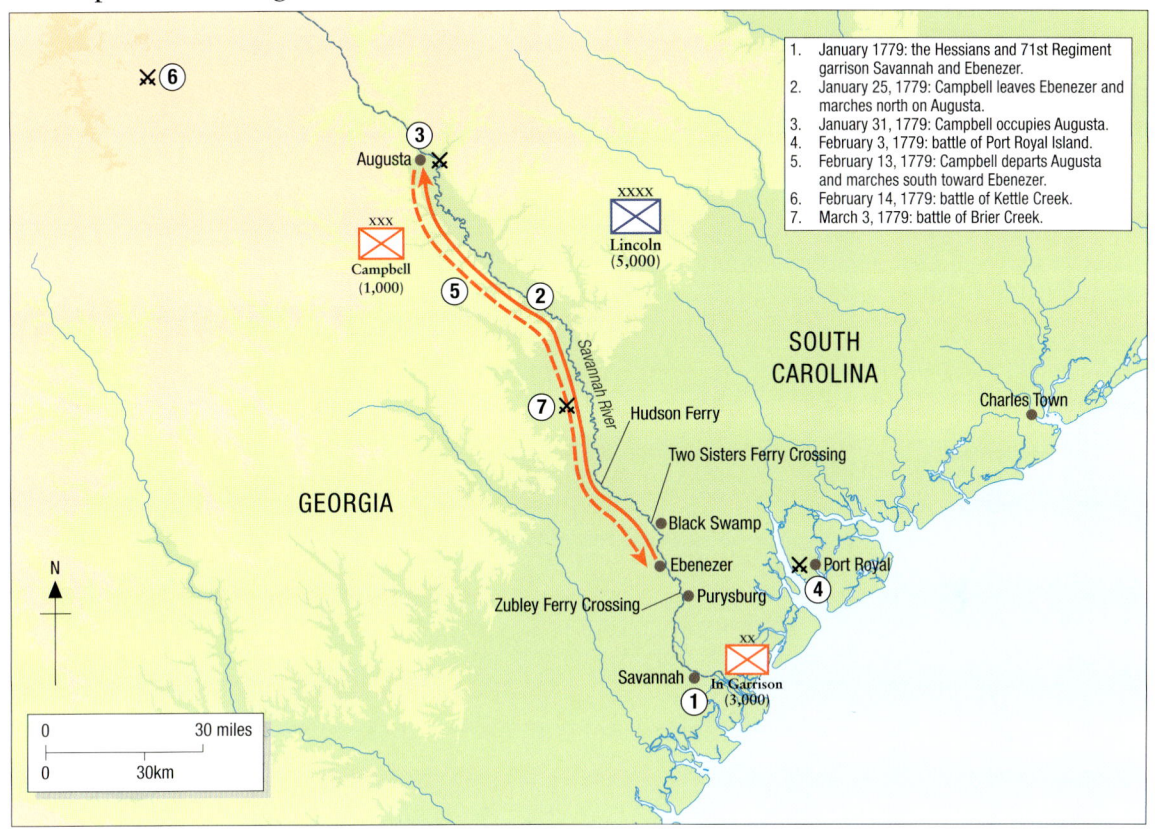

Map legend:
1. January 1779: the Hessians and 71st Regiment garrison Savannah and Ebenezer.
2. January 25, 1779: Campbell leaves Ebenezer and marches north on Augusta.
3. January 31, 1779: Campbell occupies Augusta.
4. February 3, 1779: battle of Port Royal Island.
5. February 13, 1779: Campbell departs Augusta and marches south toward Ebenezer.
6. February 14, 1779: battle of Kettle Creek.
7. March 3, 1779: battle of Brier Creek.

Although Lincoln's main force did not block Campbell's advance, various Georgia militia units under newly appointed Brigadier-General Elbert began to assemble and attempted to slow Campbell's advance. In the early morning of January 25, the Corps marched the 10 miles from Ebenezer to Hudson's Ferry. Unsure of the road condition and without any maps, Campbell sent his Light Infantry and the South Carolina Loyalists to Brier Creek, an additional 14 miles away, to secure the bridge. The militia force at the bridge had learned of the British approach and attempted to set fire to it. However the British surprised them and, following a 45-minute skirmish, forced the militia to withdraw, leaving the bridge intact. The next day a 120-man Georgia militia force assembled at the Burke County Jail to stop the British advance. Lieutenant-Colonel Thomas Brown and his rangers, along with a South Carolina militia detachment under the command of Lieutenant-Colonel Joseph Robinson, left the column to engage the rebels and free the Loyalists being held captive in the jail. On the morning of January 26, 230 Loyalists attacked, initiating an all-day skirmish. Brown withdrew leaving five of his men killed, five wounded and nine as prisoners, the Georgians lost five killed and nine wounded.

For the next several days the Corps's advance was led by Brown's mounted rangers that forced Georgia militia units to fall back and provided invaluable intelligence on road conditions and resistance encountered. On January 30, 200 Georgia militia made a determined stand to impede Campbell's advance to Fort Henderson, ten miles from Augusta. Not wanting to make a frontal assault, Campbell ordered his one howitzer and two 6lb guns to open fire on

Portion of the Kettle Creek battlefield through which Colonel Pickens' men attacked to surprise Colonel Boyd's loyalist militia encamped near the creek. (Photograph by Bernard Harris)

it. In less than ten minutes, the militia quickly withdrew and a company of the 71st Regiment crossed the creek and entered the fort. The following day, January 31, Campbell entered Augusta.

By February 3, Campbell had his force complete an abatis (a rampart of sharp wooden stakes) around several buildings and constructed a number of small redoubts in and around Augusta. Through several "confidential spies," Campbell was provided with the locations of Generals Williamson and Elbert's 1,200-man militia force, which included 300 horsemen that were positioned indirectly across the river from Augusta. Although Williamson and Elbert's main force remained on the South Carolina side of the river, they were sending out small parties across the river to harass the British and plunder suspected loyalist homes and farms. On one such foray, a group of rebel militiamen killed Private MacAlister, a very popular soldier from the 71st Light Infantry company. MacAlister had been assigned to protect the home of a Patriot militia major, who was serving his parole, and his family. Upon hearing of MacAlister's death, the men of his company swore an oath to avenge his murder. On February 8, Campbell received word of the skirmish on Port Royal Island and of a great body of men from North Carolina on their way to reinforce General Williamson. He would later learn this was Brigadier-General Ashe's North Carolina force. He also noted in his journal that Brown's Rangers and Carolina Cavalry had an extremely successful forage detail bringing in more than ten wagons of provisions and rebel ammunition. By February 10, Campbell reported that 1,100 men from the entire Province of Georgia had taken the Oath of Allegiance to the King, well short of the 6,000 men expected. The volunteers were placed in 20 companies and told of their rendezvous places in each district to assemble when needed. In addition to carrying out recruiting efforts, Campbell had his men build flat boats upon their arrival at Augusta. Following eight days of work, his men had built four flat boats that could each carry 70 men and were light enough to be transported by wagon.

As Campbell's men occupied Augusta, other events were taking place in northern Georgia and southeastern South Carolina. To draw attention away from Lieutenant-Colonel Campbell's expedition to Augusta, General Prevost directed Major William Gardner and two light companies from the 60th Regiment and one light company from the 16th Regiment totaling 160 men to capture Beaufort, South Carolina. Beaufort is located at the north end of Port Royal Island, about 30 miles northeast of Savannah and 35 miles south of Charles Town. Prevost's plan for this operation was to serve as a decoy and as a staging platform to invade South Carolina later in the year if needed. He also wanted to determine the number of Loyalists willing to support the Crown on Port Royal Island. On February 3, Gardner's force landed with the intention of capturing Beaufort. Upon hearing news of Prevost's intentions, General Lincoln directed Brigadier-General Moultrie and his South Carolina militia to block Gardner's force. Moultrie met with Brigadier Stephen Bull, the local militia district commander and nephew of former Royal Governor William Bull Jr, to develop a plan to defeat the British incursion. Bull's force quickly engaged Gardner in a short but intense skirmish that resulted in Gardner ordering a rapid 7-mile retreat to his ships. Prevost would later write of this sortie, "I am sorry to say that Major Gardner's imprudence in quitting his boats to go a place seven miles from them had nearly been the cause of the loss of the whole detachment. The retreat was cut off and but for the great bravery of the troops they [would] have been taken." Contrary to Prevost's assessment of the skirmish near Beaufort, General Moultrie wrote to Lincoln: "the enemy had gained the ground I wanted to block their route of march but determined they had already occupied the ground I wanted. It makes me happy to assure you, that our militia have that spirit which they have always been allowed to possess; nothing but discipline is wanting to make them good troops." This was the first time these South Carolina militiamen engaged British regulars, and they not only gained the upper hand, but they had also fought in the open, whereas the British were firing from bushes and trees. Following the hasty British retreat, the militiamen found nine British dead and captured five wounded, the militia lost eight men and 18 wounded. The news of this minor skirmish electrified Lincoln and his troops with the confidence that they could engage and win against the redcoats.

Nancy Hart, an American heroine who was legendary in Georgia folklore for her capture of several Loyalists in her home. She fought at Kettle Creek disguised as a man. (Library of Congress)

The other event that unfolded was Campbell sending two officers out ahead of his Augusta expedition to assemble Loyalists to join his Corps. One of the Loyalists was Colonel John Boyd, who had received his commission as a Loyalist colonel in late 1778 from General Clinton. Boyd had convinced General Clinton, while he was in New York City, that he knew the backwoods of the Carolinas, which enabled him to receive the commission and authority to raise a Loyalist militia regiment from the Carolina back-country. He was one of the Loyalist officers to sail with Campbell's expedition and, following the capture of Savannah, departed the city on January 20 and rode into the Carolinas' interior to form his Tory militia regiment. Campbell described Colonel Boyd as "a Gentleman who came a Volunteer with me from New York: and on Account of his Influence among the Back woods men of North and South Carolina, was dispatched to these Districts to collect the Loyalists and join me at Augusta." Interesting to note, Boyd had to hire a local guide to help him travel around the back-country to establish a recruiting camp and put out a call to gather Tory militia volunteers.

The second Loyalist officer sent into the back-country of Wilkes County was Major John Hamilton. The recruiting in Wilkes County was brutal because Hamilton believed that anyone who did not join him deserved to be punished. Colonel John Dooley and Lieutenant-Colonel Elijah Clarke of the Wilkes Country militia lacked the manpower to deal with Hamilton, so they appealed to South Carolina for help. In response, Colonel Andrew Pickens and his men soon arrived and forced Hamilton and his Loyalists to be contained in Carr's Fort. Pickens' initial plan was to burn the Loyalists out but, when he was informed that there were women and children in the fort and there was no available water, he decided on a siege of the fort instead. He rationalized that Hamilton would eventually call for a surrender because of their lack of water. As the siege continued, word came that Colonel Boyd and his men were riding through South Carolina enroute to Augusta, threatening families, taking provisions, and destroying homes as they traveled. Several homes belonged to Pickens' men and, fearing for their families' safety, most of his 350 men rode toward the town of Ninety-Six to intercept Boyd. Once Major Hamilton realized most of Pickens' force had departed, he was able to evacuate Carr's Fort and return to Augusta.

BATTLE OF KETTLE CREEK

Boyd's inexperienced Tory militia force, composed of 800 men from the Carolinas, rode 150 miles through the back-country of the Carolinas to join with Campbell's force at Augusta. His force looted and pillaged along its march, increasing the animosity toward Loyalists. After several skirmishes with various Patriot forces, Colonel Boyd rested his reduced force of 700 men in Georgia along the flooded Kettle Creek, a tributary of the Savannah River, some 50 miles northwest of Augusta. Not knowing the location of Pickens' force, Boyd sent his men's horses out to pasture to rest, as his militia settled into a temporary camp. The area for his encampment consisted of rolling and dissecting wooded ridges with a very limited plain area. Around 10.00am on February 14, Pickens' force marched 3 miles to approach Boyd's camp, and then divided into three groups to launch its attack. Dooley commanded the right wing and Clarke, the left wing, each consisting of 100 men, while

Pickens led the 200-man-strong center group, along with an advance guard. Startled by the attack from the rear of their camp, Boyd quickly assembled 100 men to a fence and fallen timber line to meet the threat. Boyd briefly managed to hold but, seeing his precarious position, ordered a retreat to the higher ground north of Kettle Creek; however as they withdrew, Boyd fell mortally wounded. Temporarily leaderless, Boyd's untrained militia fell apart and many escaped across the flooded Kettle Creek, abandoning their camp equipment and horses. The main American attack came from Clarke's left wing, which eventually broke the Loyalists' line. Although Loyalist Major William Spurgeon was able to rally and hold a number of survivors together to perform a disciplined retreat, the battle ended in a clear Patriot victory. Boyd lost 70 killed, 75 wounded and 150 captured. Pickens' force also captured 600 horses and a considerable amount of baggage. Pickens' force suffered nine killed and 23 wounded and freed over 30 prisoners captured in previous skirmishes. Several Loyalist prisoners stayed behind for the burial party and were granted paroles as the rest were taken to Augusta, which had recently been vacated by Campbell. On February 16, Colonel Pickens wrote a letter to his superior, General Andrew Williamson, to tell him of the victory at Kettle Creek and that he was taking the prisoners to Ninety-Six, South Carolina for trial. Seventy were sentenced to be hanged because of their plundering and criminal actions during their 150-mile march through South Carolina, but only five sentences were actually carried out.

Congreve's 3lb "Grasshopper" cannon replica. The cannon used by both sides gave the infantry a heavier-caliber weapon when compared with the musket in the open field. Heavy cannons were needed against entrenched or fortified positions. (Coastal Heritage Society)

The day prior to Kettle Creek, Campbell reassembled his forces back to Augusta and began their march to Ebenezer. On the fourth day after departing Augusta, his Corps encamped near Brier Creek, Georgia, halfway between Augusta and Savannah and was joined by 270 North Carolina Loyalists who had escaped the debacle at Kettle Creek. During this time, General Lincoln ordered Brigadier-General John Ashe's North Carolina Brigade, which had recently arrived at Purysburg from eastern North Carolina, to intercept Campbell's force. Upon hearing of the British withdrawal, Ashe moved northwest along the Savannah River and crossed at Augusta and then followed the British route southeast along the river. The evening of February 20, Campbell's Corps reached Hudson's Ferry, 23 miles from Ebenezer. Campbell wrote of his dismay that there was no rum waiting for his "brave fellows" despite his repeated letters to Prevost for that support. In addition, he was met by Lieutenant-Colonel James Prevost with orders to assume command of his Corps, since his request to return home to his estate in Scotland had been approved. During their handover, Campbell shared his sketch of the area along the road to Augusta and informed Prevost of the current state of the Corps. Campbell also suggested to Prevost that the Rebels could be surprised near Brier Creek if their main force was to advance that far. He recommended a force to march around their position and hit them from behind while conducting a feint demonstration to their front and drive them into the Savannah River. Ashe took his time from February 27 to March 2 to assemble his North Carolina militia and Georgia militia to establish a defensive position along Brier Creek, near Campbell's force. Across the river from his position at Matthews Bluff were General Rutherford's 700 men and several cannons, whose intent was to build a bridge and join forces with Ashe.

On February 24, Campbell, along with Captain Tawes and his dragoons, rode to Ebenezer to meet with General Prevost, who had been promoted in early February. Campbell gave Prevost an account of his expedition to Augusta, along with the handover of his command to his younger brother James. Two days later General Prevost and Lieutenant-Colonel Archibald Campbell departed for Savannah to meet with Commodore Parker and discuss the subject of restoring a civil government in Georgia. Campbell recommended that authority be granted to Lieutenant-Colonel James Prevost to serve as the interim governor until former Royal Governor Wright returned from Britain, thereby removing a stripe from the American flag.

By February 28, General Lincoln had assembled an army exceeding 5,000 men. He positioned between 3,000 and 4,000 men at Purysburg, General Ashe's force of about 1,000 was on the west side of the Savannah River near Brier Creek, General Rutherford's 800 men were at Black Swamp, South Carolina and General Williamson's 1,200 men near Augusta. Lincoln held a council of war at his Black Swamp headquarters with Ashe and Williamson to discuss their next move. Ashe assured him his position at Brier Creek was strong and Lincoln agreed to move the majority of his force and Williamson's to join Ashe, with the intention of cutting off and destroying the British force near Brier Creek. They had learned through deserters and locals that Lieutenant-Colonel Prevost was now in command of Campbell's Corps.

BATTLE OF BRIER CREEK

On March 2, James Prevost carried out Campbell's recommendation and nearly 400 men of the 1st Battalion 71st Regiment took up positions across the Brier Creek as a show of force to divert the American attention to their front. The remainder of the force, about 900 British and Tory militia, had departed to make an overnight march around Ashe's force. The flanking column, led by Lieutenant-Colonel John Maitland, consisted of his 2nd Battalion 71st Regiment, which had recently marched from Ebenezer, 40 men on captured horses, two companies of light infantry, three companies of the 60th Royal American Regiment and 50 men from Brown's Rangers. As Maitland's force got into attack position on March 3, the British had caught Ashe's force, unaware that it was trapped between the mosquito-infested Brier Creek and Savannah River.

Around 3.00pm, Maitland's flanking column attacked. His right flank consisted of Captain Baird's light infantry, his center by the 2nd Battalion 71st Regiment along with the five artillery pieces, and his left flank by North Carolina Loyalists. Maitland held the 60th companies along with Captain Tawes's dragoons in reserve. A screen of 50 riflemen had been set up to shoot any militia attempting to reach the Savannah River. The attack took the Patriots completely by surprise, although Ashe was able to turn his regiments around to get into a line of battle to meet the oncoming attack. The Georgia Continentals, holding the center, managed to fire two volleys but then without orders moved forward, creating a gap between them and the North Carolina (Edenton) militia on their right flank. The 2nd Battalion 71st Regiment saw the gap and charged. Ashe's center soon collapsed, but his left flank, composed of additional North Carolina militia, continued to hold. Ashe's subordinate commanders, General Samuel Elbert and Lieutenant-Colonel John McIntosh managed to rally some Continental and militia troops and continue fighting until they were overwhelmed. The entire engagement lasted only about 15 minutes and within the first five minutes, after the initial volleys, most of Ashe's force had fled. Realizing the fight was over, Ashe rode away and crossed the Savannah River in a rowboat to join General Rutherford at Matthews Bluff. Reports would eventually reach him revealing that between 50 and 100 men drowned attempting to cross the Savannah River. His total losses included 150 soldiers killed and wounded and over 200 captured; in comparison, the British lost one officer, five men killed and ten wounded.

Captain Edward Rutledge, younger brother of Governor Rutledge, and signatory for South Carolina of the Declaration of Independence. He participated in the February 3, 1779 battle on Port Royal Island. (State Archives of Florida)

A court martial was convened the following week, starting on March 13 near Lincoln's headquarters at Purysburg. Even though General Ashe was found not guilty, he was found to have left his camp unsecured and had not taken the appropriate means to gather intelligence about the enemy's location. Ashe would later write, "never was an army more completely surprised, and never were men more panic struck, the poor fellows!" General Lincoln had sent a written request to General Prevost to provide him with an account of the number of Patriot prisoners and officers taken at Brier Creek, which included 162 rank-and-file prisoners and 24 officers. As the court-martial inquiry convened on March 16, Lieutenant-Colonel Campbell embarked on the HMS *Phoenix* at Savannah and soon departed America never to return. He eventually reached Plymouth, England on May 14.

Following the destruction of Ashe's force, a distraught Lincoln gathered his commanders for a council of war to discuss their next course of action and agreed to gather their forces in and around Purysburg to counter any British moves across the river. Lincoln spent the next six weeks requesting supplies, encouraging militia units to extend past their three-month enlistments, and solicited the governors of North Carolina and Virginia for three-month militia volunteers. A highlight for Lincoln occurred in early April when General Williamson and his militia defeated a large band of Creeks and Cherokees in western South Carolina, preventing all but a few Native Americans from reaching the British forces at Ebenezer. Williamson's actions helped to quell Lincoln's concern about the Georgia and Carolina militias' ability to defend their homes in the back-country and thwarted any further attempts by the British to influence the tribes to carry out summer raids.

On April 5, General Lincoln gave Williamson, encamped near Black Swamp about 25 miles north of Purysburg, the instruction to make incursions into Georgia whenever possible, to harass or annoy the enemy. A week later,

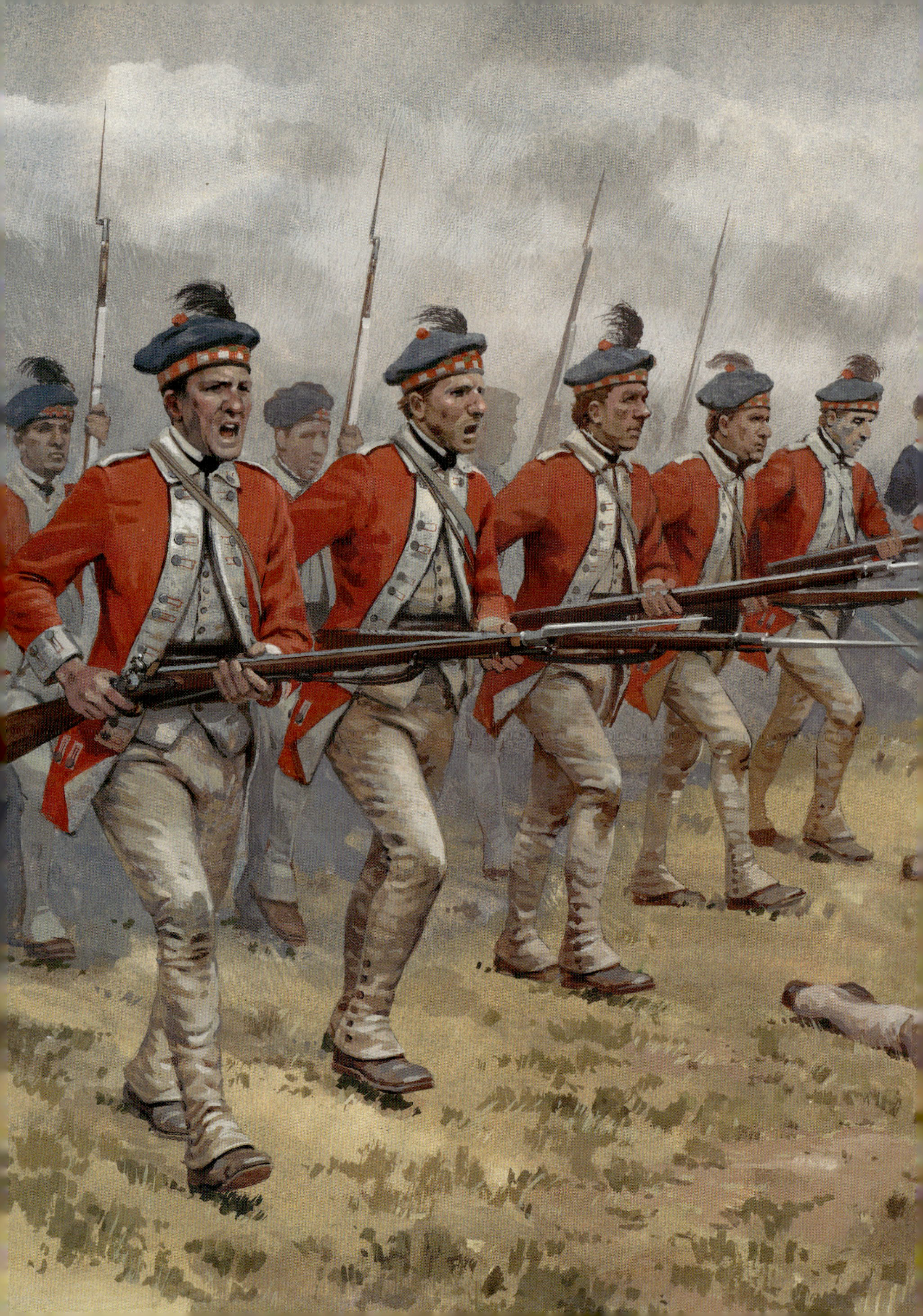

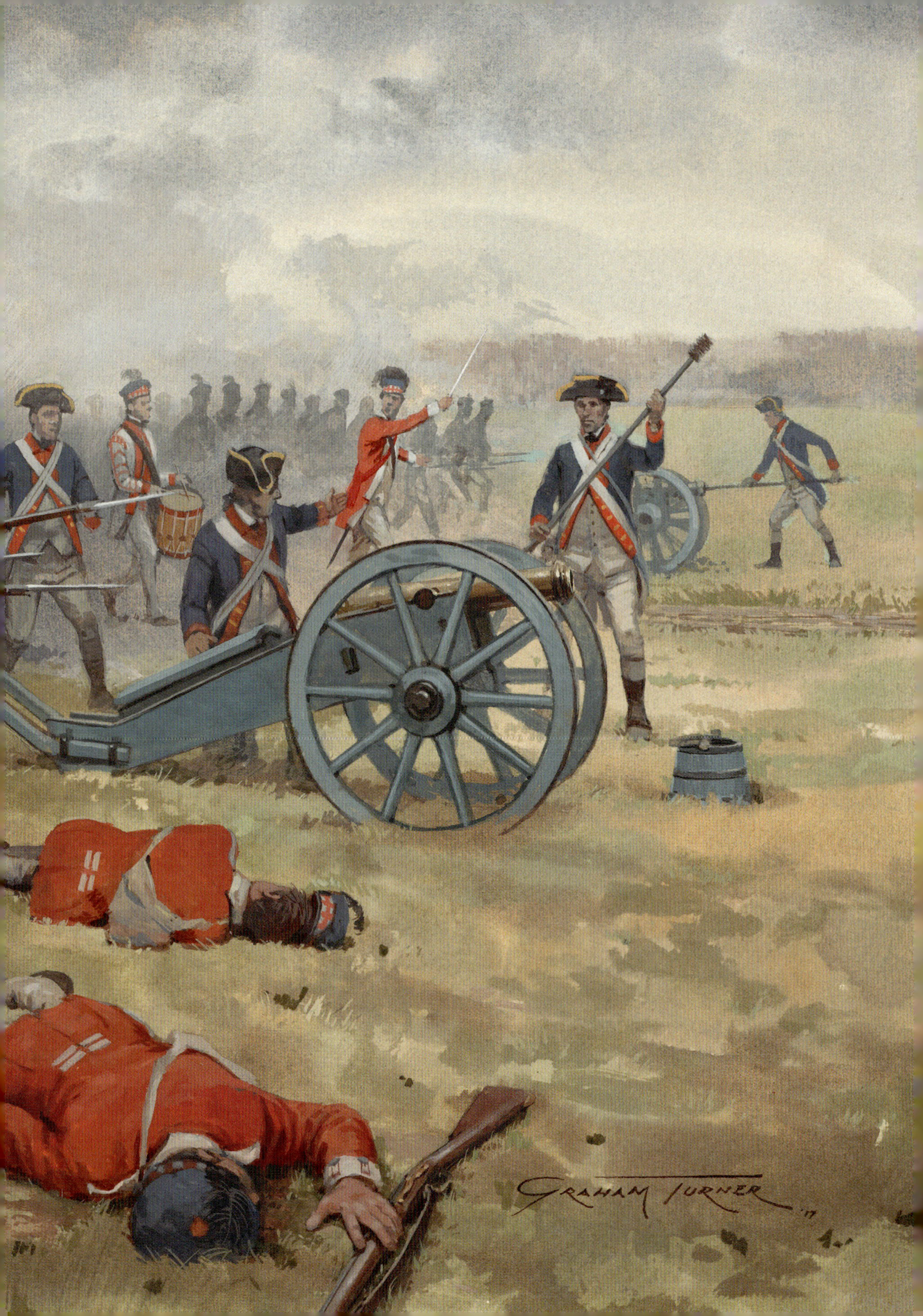
GRAHAM TURNER

BATTLE OF BRIER CREEK, MARCH 3, 1779 (PP. 54–55)

Around 3pm on March 3, the British flanking column led by the 2nd Battalion 71st Highland Regiment (1), along with five cannon (2), attacked Brigadier-General Ashe's North Carolinians and Georgians. The attack took Ashe's command by surprise and they attempted to get into a ragged line of battle to meet the oncoming force. The Georgia Continentals holding the center managed to fire two volleys but they moved forward creating a gap between them and the North Carolina (Edenton) Militia on their right flank. The highlanders saw the opportunity and charged home, several of whom yelled "Now boys, remember poor MacAlister." For many of the Americans, this was their first encounter with the British Redcoats and many of the defenders turned and ran without firing a shot. Ashe's left flank comprised of other North Carolina militia continued to hold for a short period until they were overwhelmed. Patriot leaders Brigadier-General Samuel Elbert and Lieutenant-Colonel John McIntosh (commander at Sunbury fort in November) had rallied some Continental and militia troops to form a ragtag reserve line until they were overwhelmed as well, both of whom would be captured. The engagement only lasted about 15 minutes but significantly changed Major-General Lincoln's future plans against the British.

Lincoln wrote to James Lovell, his friend and Massachusetts congressional delegate, summarizing the state of his forces and requesting to be relieved. Lincoln wrote, "I have been too long accustomed to a Northern climate to think of risquing a seasoning at this time of life to a southern one. I hope my friends will not suffer me to be kept here long." Lincoln had sent his aide Everard Meade with the dispatches, along with first-hand accounts of the Southern Department situation. Meade, at Lincoln's request, would lobby members of Congress in private and disclose Lincoln's concern that his wound from Saratoga would prove fatal if he remained in South Carolina during the summer.

On April 19, Lincoln held another council of war with his commanders, Generals Moultrie, Huger, and Sumner to discuss their next move. He informed them that, in addition to their forces, the promised 500 South Carolina militia from Orangeburg, and 700 men were coming from North Carolina so along with General Williamson's force there would be 5,000 men. He sought their approval for his plan to march north and cross the Savannah River near Augusta to secure it and the Georgia back-country against any remaining Loyalist forces. He claimed this would prevent or at least limit the number of supplies from the region from reaching the British, as well as further ensure the Creek and Cherokee Native Americans did not attempt to join Prevost. A force of about 1,000 militia and 220 South Carolina Continentals would remain near Purysburg under Moultrie's command to watch and deny the Savannah River crossing sites near Ebenezer and Hudson Ferry. The next day, Lincoln's army marched northwest toward Augusta. Upon hearing of this movement many South Carolina assembly members questioned Lincoln's decision and motives and worried about a British incursion into their state.

EXPEDITION TO CHARLES TOWN

The British supply situation in and around Savannah continued to deteriorate because of the lack of provisions from the Georgia hinterland and unreliable shipping schedules. As the military commander in Georgia, General Prevost needed provisions (beef and rice) to support his 4,000-man force, along with the residents of Savannah. As word of Lincoln's march northward reached his headquarters from his rangers and deserters, he grabbed the opportunity to cross the Savannah River into South Carolina. On April 28, over 2,000 British, Hessian and loyalist troops along with 70 Native Americans, the majority of whom were Seminoles, crossed into South Carolina. British Major Francis John Skelly wrote, "British Army under Maj. Gen. Prevost left Ebenezer. First division consisting of the Light Infantry and two Batt [battalions] 71st Reg embarked in flat Boats cross'd the Savannah River four miles below Purisburg [Purysburg], entered swamps that Evening---All night wading thro' them. At Sunrise arrived on dry ground two miles from Purysburg. The honorable Lieutenant-Colonel Maitland commanding the first division, he attacked the town (which was poorly defended) took it by 10 o'clock this morning." On April 30, Skelly further wrote, "the remainder of the Army arrived at Purysburg, they consisted of two troops of Dragoons, Grenadier company of the 60th Regiment, two battalions of Hessians, New York Volunteers, one battalion of DeLancy's, part of Skinners Regiment,

The expedition to Charles Town

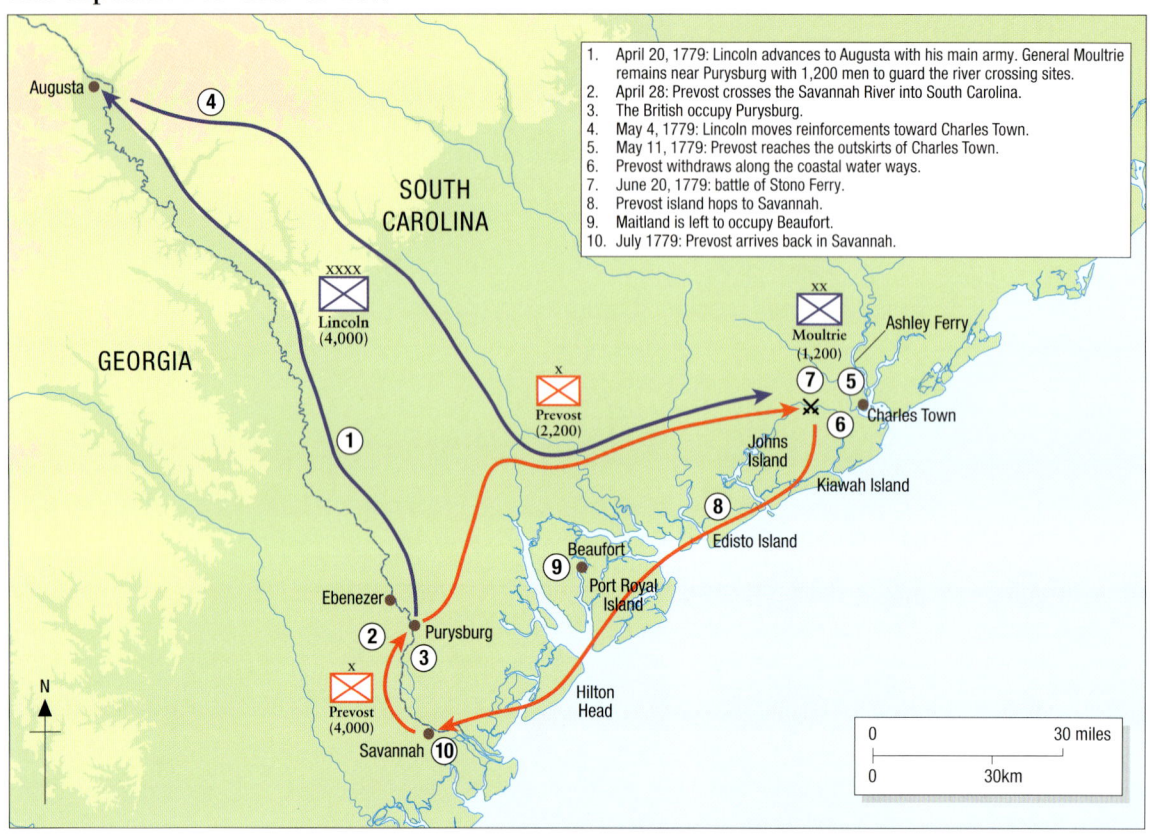

1. April 20, 1779: Lincoln advances to Augusta with his main army. General Moultrie remains near Purysburg with 1,200 men to guard the river crossing sites.
2. April 28: Prevost crosses the Savannah River into South Carolina.
3. The British occupy Purysburg.
4. May 4, 1779: Lincoln moves reinforcements toward Charles Town.
5. May 11, 1779: Prevost reaches the outskirts of Charles Town.
6. Prevost withdraws along the coastal water ways.
7. June 20, 1779: battle of Stono Ferry.
8. Prevost island hops to Savannah.
9. Maitland is left to occupy Beaufort.
10. July 1779: Prevost arrives back in Savannah.

two small Corps of Carolinians … and some irregulars [Native Americans], a detachment of Artillery, eight light field pieces and a small howitzer … marched this evening to Turkey Hill." On April 30, Moultrie received a letter from one of his commanders, Colonel Alex McIntosh, that several deserters from Maitland's light company informed him that they were in advance of over 1,500 men. Moultrie now had a better appreciation of the size of force he was dealing with as the British advanced farther into South Carolina.

In the meantime, on May 1 Lincoln called for a new Georgia legislature to meet in Augusta as part of his plan to "give a new existence to the State of Georgia." Lincoln, while camped at Augusta, informed Moultrie that help was on the way, but would not send his entire force until Prevost's intentions were determined. He dispatched 300 Continentals to join Moultrie as Governor Rutledge sent more militia to Charles Town. As the British advanced farther into South Carolina, their actions would be considered a rampage rather than a march by a disciplined army. They pillaged and destroyed along the route of march, confiscating all food supplies with no distinction between friend or foe. On May 3, Moultrie wrote to Governor Rutledge, "I am sorry to inform you, the enemy with parties of horse and Indians, are ravaging the country in a barbarous manner, killing people and burning a number of houses as they go on." That same day, Lieutenant-Colonel John Laurens, a 24-year-old and aggressive officer, on his own initiative, decided to make a stand against the advancing British. Moultrie had provided Laurens, his rearguard commander, with specific instructions about pulling his force across the Coosawhatchie River, but contrary to his commander's intentions Laurens kept his men on the near side of the river to engage the British. His impulsive decision cost his command a number of casualties and failed to slow the British advance. Despite this setback, Moultrie continued to gather intelligence through deserters and was able to surmise that Prevost had under 3,000 men under his command but still remained unclear of Prevost's true intentions.

In response to Moultrie's letter, Governor Rutledge sent out a proclamation calling upon all inhabitants along Prevost's route to Charles Town to rise and resist the redcoats. His plea went unanswered as many of the militia deserted to protect their homesteads or to flee with their families. As Moultrie's army continued to withdraw, he received confirmation that Prevost did intend to capture Charles Town and then notified Lincoln and Rutledge. To continue to impede the progress of Prevost's advance, a number of bridges and watercraft were either burned or dismantled and trees were cut down along the road, but the British quickly rebuilt some bridges under the guidance of their engineering officer, Captain James Moncrief. Moultrie would write of this period:

> There never was a country in greater confusion and consternation … five armies … marching through the southern parts of it at the same time, and all for different purposes: myself, retreating as fast as possible to get into town [Charles Town]; the British army of three thousand men … in pursuit of me; and General Lincoln with the American army of four thousand marching with hasty strides to come up with the British; Governor Rutledge from Orangeburg with about six hundred militia, hastening to get into town [Charles Town] lest he should be shut out, and Colonel Harris [of Georgia] with a detachment of 250 Continentals pushing on with all possible dispatch to reinforce me … In short, it was nothing but a general confusion and alarm.

At Ashley Ferry, 7 miles from the South Carolina capital, a number of boats and ferries were confiscated by the British. On May 11, lead elements of Prevost's army had reached the outskirts of Charles Town, while Lieutenant-Colonel Maitland kept a force at Ashley Ferry. Later that day, Captain Tawes's dragoons and Major Gardner's light infantry engaged Pulaski's legion. Pulaski positioned his infantry behind a breastwork and advanced with his cavalry to meet the British. The British dragoons and infantry charge pushed Pulaski's men from their positions, inflicting over 50 casualties on his legion, whereas Tawes lost six men. As the British closed on Charles Town, Moncrief advised Prevost that the American defensive works were "impregnable without heavy artillery" which they did not have.

South Carolina Governor John Rutledge constantly asked the Continental Congress for more men, supplies, and funding. At odds with General Lincoln on numerous occasions, it was his letter on June 1779, however, that convinced Lincoln not to resign and to continue to serve as the Southern Department commander. (Library of Congress)

Africans fought for both sides during the war as slaves and as free men. There were only two identifiable African units: the 1st Rhode Island Regiment (pictured) and the Chasseurs-Volontaires de Saint-Domingue. (Anne S.K. Brown Military Collection)

As events unfolded later that day, Governor Rutledge and the majority of the eight-member South Carolina Privy (assembly) wanted to negotiate terms of neutrality with General Prevost and ordered General Moultrie to send a messenger with that request. Rutledge and members of the Privy believed the greater concern was for the welfare of the South Carolina citizens and their property over independence from Britain and unity with the other 12 colonial states. Based on that position, Rutledge sent his request to General Prevost, which read, "To propose neutrality, during the war between Great Britain and America, and the question, whether the state shall belong to Great Britain, or remain one of the United States be determined by the treaty of peace between those two powers." In response, Prevost sent his brother James Prevost with his reply, stating that his business was with General Moultrie, the military commander, since the garrison was under arms and must surrender as prisoners of war. Moultrie had four hours to decide the fate of the city. Moultrie, along with his military commanders, Pulaski and Lieutenant-Colonel Laurens, strongly supported the defense of the city. Although they believed their forces were outnumbered by the British, they felt they could hold the city's defensive works until Lincoln's army arrived. Moultrie was quoted as saying, "we will fight it out." In reality, Prevost had only 1,400 troops outside the city with the remaining 1,200 troops under Maitland's command 7 miles away at Ashley Ferry; this compared with Moultrie's 2,500 defenders, many of whom were militia. Moultrie informed his staff, the governor and Privy members that his decision was to fight and defend Charles Town. General Prevost's bluff was called and with no other option, since he did not have the time, troops, or the heavy-caliber cannons to attack or conduct a siege, ordered his forces to withdraw. That evening, Major Skelly noted, "we heard a false alarm in Town and the defenders fired a great many canon, discharged a volley of musketry at their own patriots [and] killed a Major Huger [Benjamin Huger, brother of General Isaac Huger] and twenty of their own people."

The dilemma Prevost now faced was that he was over 100 miles away from his base of operations and was encountering an enemy force determined to fight from fortified positions, and was in receipt of a captured dispatch announcing Lincoln's rapid march to Charles Town. He knew the route he was taking to Charles Town was not feasible, since it would not provide him with the security or resources his army would need, since it had been ransacked by his troops. Prevost determined his best option was to withdraw along the South Carolina coastal waterways by utilizing the ferries and boats captured at Ashley Ferry and those along the waterways. He also planned to accumulate additional provisions along the way and sail them back to Savannah. His army would use the islands along the route as encampments, while boats would ferry his force from island to island. As the British slipped away, Moultrie and city officials were panicked over the next several days about their exact location; rumors spread quickly that an amphibious assault on Charles Town was imminent. It was not until May 17 that Lincoln (at Parker's Ferry) finally learned the exact location of Prevost's force from prisoners and from reports by Pulaski's cavalry detachments. Prior to this confirmation, additional forces had been sent to Fort Moultrie on Sullivan Island and other coastal areas around Charles Town to provide reinforcement, since they expected a British attack from the sea.

The British continued to loot and torch plantations and homes as they withdrew to James Island. One of the plantations plundered was Governor Rutledge's. He emotionally urged Lincoln to crush those "Thieves, Robbers & Plunderers" once and for all. By May 19, British forces were stretched along the Stono River from Wapoo Cut to the Stono Ferry site. On May 26, Lincoln was at Ashley Ferry and learned from Colonel Pulaski the exact deployment of British forces around Stono Ferry on James Island. Based on Pulaski's recent report, Lincoln held a council of war with General Moultrie and his other commanders. They devised a plan to make a frontal attack on the British positions for June 1, while using Moultrie's force to swing around from James Island to attack from the rear. Pulaski soon added more information to the effect that the British were consolidating and entrenching their forces on James Island to cover the Stono Ferry site, which they were using as a point of departure for foraging parties. Lincoln decided to wait about six miles from the ferry site with his army, to watch and wait for another opportunity to attack.

On June 8 Lincoln received a dispatch from Congress that his request for recall from the Southern Department was confirmed. The next day, Lincoln wrote to inform Rutledge and Moultrie of his permission to resign. Moultrie had also received a letter from the President of Congress promoting him to major-general and giving him command of the Southern Department upon Lincoln's departure. Moultrie immediately replied to Lincoln's letter pleading with him to stay as their commander. Lincoln's reply to Moultrie reflected his despair at what he had achieved as the Southern Department commander, "as it appears, from unkind declarations daily thrown out in your Capital [Charles Town], that I have lost that confidence of this people ... I ought to retire ... A man should sacrifice his own feelings to his country's good." Although Moultrie pleaded with him to stay, it was Rutledge's letter on June 13 that convinced Lincoln. Rutledge confirmed with the South Carolina assembly

4th South Carolina artillery train driver who would have participated in engagements from Savannah to Stono Ferry. (Anness Publishing Ltd)

that they wanted Lincoln as their commander. The South Carolina governor wrote, "character, and knowledge and Experience in the Art of War are such, and the publick [public] has so much Confidence in you, that your remaining here will ensure great good to this, and the Neighboring state [Georgia]." Now reassured, Lincoln decided to stay.

On June 10, Prevost split his force and accompanied the advance force to scout the approaches to Savannah. He left his brother, Lieutenant-Colonel Prevost, to maintain the bridgehead at Stono Ferry, 18 miles from Charles Town on the John's Island crossing site. On June 16, General Prevost ordered his brother to depart Stono Ferry with half of the 1,600-man force and join him farther downstream. The Stono Ferry bridgehead site was left to the command of Lieutenant-Colonel Maitland of the 71st Highland Regiment. Maitland's command at Stono Ferry consisted of 350 men of the 1st Battalion of 71st Highlanders, 200 Hessians from the Wissenbach regiment, and 250 North Carolina Volunteers (many of whom fought at Kettle Creek) and 1st Battalion of South Carolina Loyalists. Maitland positioned his force to hold his bridgehead until ordered to move south and rejoin the main army. The British center was held by Lieutenant-Colonel John Hamilton's North and South Carolina loyalist militia, his right flank by the 1st Battalion 71st Regiment and the left flank by the Hessian regiment.

BATTLE OF STONO FERRY

On the evening of June 19, Lincoln received new intelligence that a force of only 600 British and their allies would soon depart Stono Ferry and that their fortifications were not as strong as had been reported and corroborated by deserters. Lincoln held a council of war with his commanders and decided to attack the next morning with a flanking move by Moultrie on James Island in an attempt to distract Maitland and destroy his supplies across the Stono River. A contributing factor to their decision to attack, rather than let Maitland depart of his own accord, was that many North Carolina and Virginia militia enlistments were set to expire, and if they did not take offensive action against the British they believed that would directly exacerbate the growing desertion and morale problems. Lincoln immediately ordered Lieutenant-Colonel Henderson to march his light infantry battalion the 3 miles from camp to secure the route of march and screen the army from Maitland's force. Upon hearing of the pending attack, Lincoln was pleasantly surprised to see the dramatic shift in the spirit and enthusiasm of his troops to finally see action rather than sitting idle in camp for the past month.

The next morning around 7.00am the sun was up and it promised to be another hot day. Lincoln had assembled his 1,500 men about 300–400 yards from Maitland's entrenched line into two attacking wings and then launched his attack. His left wing was under the command of South Carolina native, Brigadier-General Isaac Huger, consisting of the North and South Carolina Continental brigades. The right wing, composed of the Carolina militia regiments, was under the command of General Jethro Sumner, a former North Carolina tavern owner and veteran of Brandywine Creek and Germantown. Colonel David Mason's Virginia militia battalion and Lieutenant-Colonel Daniel Horry's South Carolina light horse were held in reserve. Colonel Owen Robert's 4th South Carolina artillery, consisting of eight 4lb guns, would support the attack. Moultrie's command would cross over to the northern end of John's Island and threaten the rear of the British. Lincoln's alignment ensured his most experienced troops under Huger's command would attack the 71st Highland Regiment, Maitland's best troops. Maitland's bridgehead sat in the middle of an empty field stretching about a half-mile along the Stono River with the road to the ferry splitting his bridgehead in half. About 100 yards on either side of the road were square earthwork redoubts and 400 yards farther on his right flank was a round redoubt and entrenchments, each of the redoubts could hold up to 40 men. In addition, abatis were erected in front of his entrenchments with clear fields of fire. Maitland's five small cannons and one howitzer were posted near the redoubts and road. Lincoln's plan called for Sumner's right wing to attack first with the intention of drawing British forces from their right flank to reinforce their left. Huger's attack would then, if all went according to plan, hit a weaker British right flank. However, as Sumner's force began its 2-mile march to its attack position in the early morning light it was slowed on account of the thick undergrowth and densely wooded area. Meanwhile, Huger's force advanced more expeditiously, since the forest it marched through was clear of brush, although a half-mile from the British line its lead units ran into two light companies of the 71st deployed as a screen for a possible attack. The brief skirmish between the light troops caught Maitland's attention, but he was not sure if the firing was a signal of a major attack or just another of the skirmishes between detachments and forage parties that had occurred on previous occasions over the past week. Huger's force quickly overwhelmed the two companies and pursued them until they came to within 300 yards of the entrenchments. As Huger's Continentals closed on the abatis and entrenchments they were startled to see a marshy creek that ran in front of the British far right flank. As the Continentals came within musketry range, they were met by a withering musket volley and canister fire from the 71st Highlanders and their supporting cannon. The Continentals hesitated to continue their advance and instead traded volley fire with the British behind their entrenchments and redoubt. Meanwhile as Huger's advance outpaced the right wing, General Sumner eventually was able to deploy his militia regiments into a line of battle stretching almost 700 yards from the road to the Stono River. A militia officer recorded the encounter of the his unit's advance, "The British reserved their fire till we were within sixty yards of their positions when a general discharge of musket and artillery fire checked our progress." The militia performed as their Continental counterparts did on their left flank and traded volley fires against the Hessians and Loyalists. Following the battle, a British officer noted that the attack was "supported by the provincials with more than usual firmness." As the firing on the British extreme left flank held by the Hessians slackened, Colonel Malmady's light infantry, composed of a number of Continentals, charged home. The Hessians broke and ran. Seeing that his 71st was firmly holding the right flank and Huger's men showed no signs of advancing, Maitland quickly ordered several companies of Highlanders to plug the gap vacated by the Hessians. Maitland was then able to rally the Hessians and join in the counterattack. As Malmady's troops breached the far left British entrenchments, Lincoln and Huger were completely unaware of Malmady's success as they continued to inspire their men to assault the entrenchments but to no avail. Sumner believed if the reserve had been sent to his wing, they would have been

BRITISH UNITS
A. 71st Regiment
B. North and South Carolina Provincials
C. Wissenbach Regiment
D. Companies of 71st Regiment

MAITLAND

STONO RIVER

MAINLAND LANDING

JOHNS ISLAND LANDING

71ST REGIMENT ENCAMPMENT

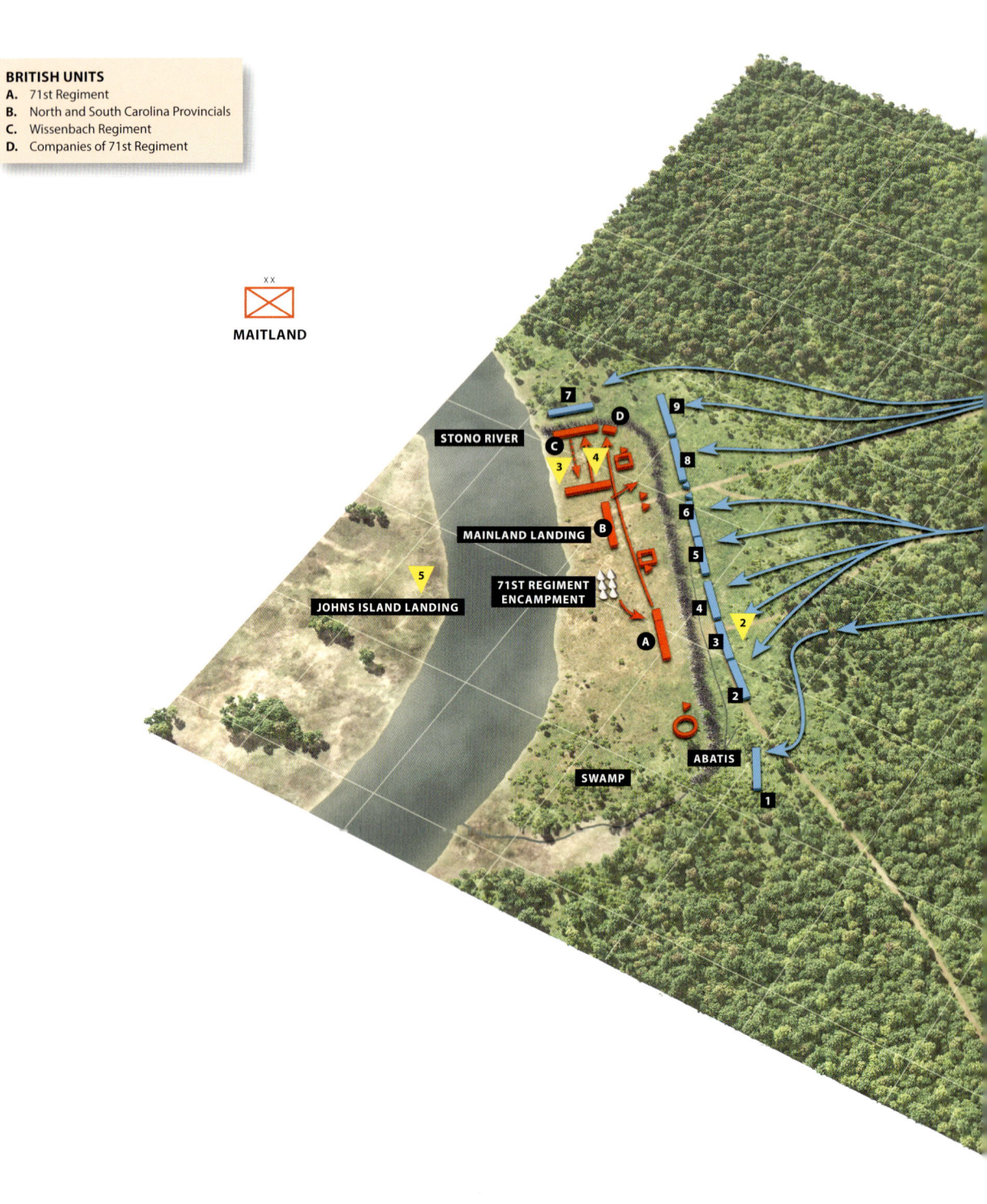

SWAMP

ABATIS

EVENTS

1. The American 2nd Light Infantry overrun British skirmishers.
2. American attack British right flank.
3. Wissenbach Hessian regiment forced to retreat.
4. Companies of 71st and rallied Hessians counterattack Malmady.
5. British reinforcements appear on Johns Island.
6. Lincoln withdraws.

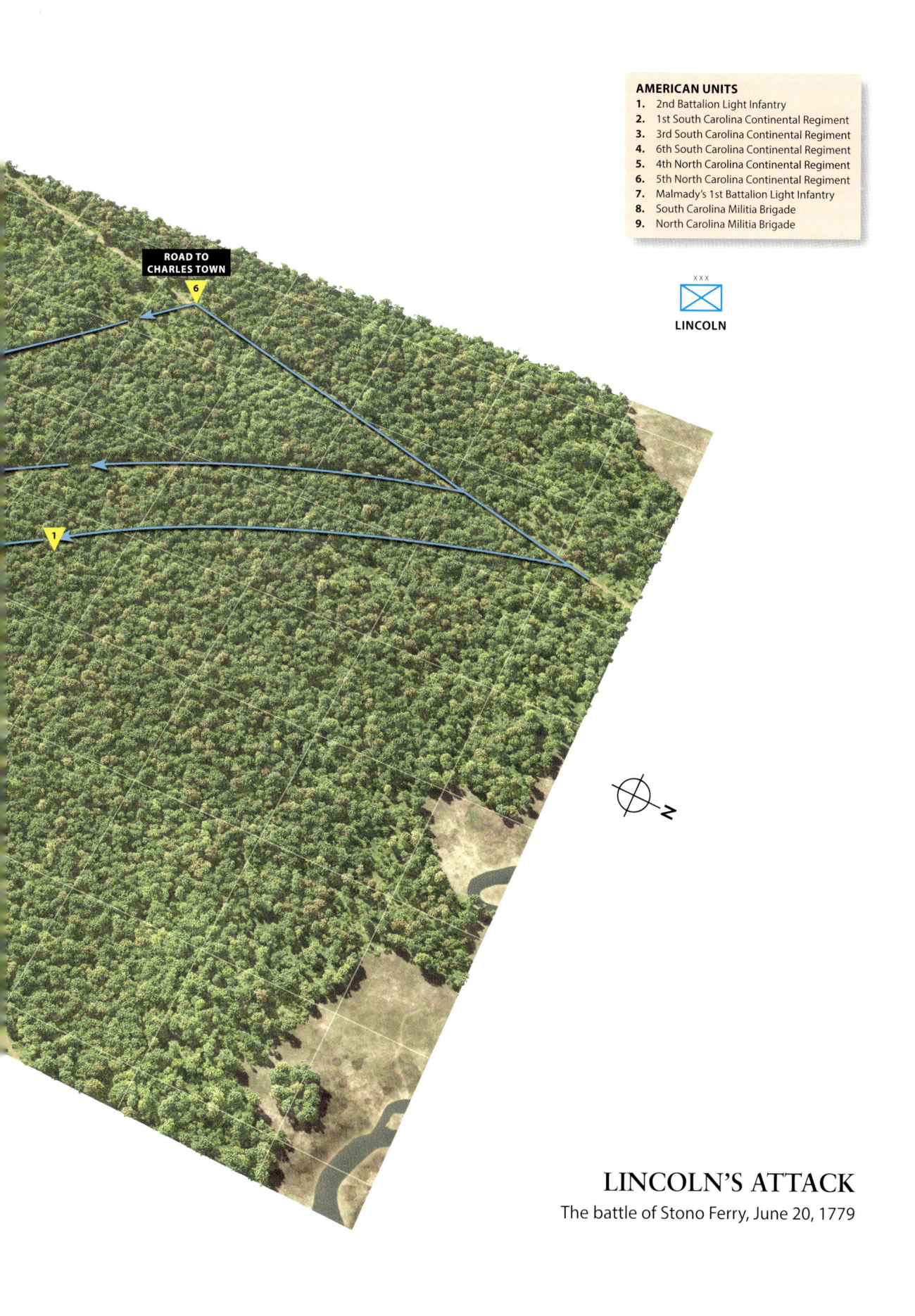

AMERICAN UNITS
1. 2nd Battalion Light Infantry
2. 1st South Carolina Continental Regiment
3. 3rd South Carolina Continental Regiment
4. 6th South Carolina Continental Regiment
5. 4th North Carolina Continental Regiment
6. 5th North Carolina Continental Regiment
7. Malmady's 1st Battalion Light Infantry
8. South Carolina Militia Brigade
9. North Carolina Militia Brigade

ROAD TO CHARLES TOWN

LINCOLN

LINCOLN'S ATTACK
The battle of Stono Ferry, June 20, 1779

able to roll up the entire British left flank. The determination of the British counterattack pushed Malmady's men back to their starting point. By 8.30am Lincoln realized his attack has been repulsed, and observed his 4lb cannons had little to no effect on the British redoubts or entrenchments. Moreover, he was getting reports of the 2nd Battalion, 71st Regiment marching towards the ferry, coming from the southern end of John's Island. With a chance of victory gone, Lincoln ordered a withdrawal. A tragic moment occurred at this point when his artillery commander, Colonel Owen Roberts, an officer who was much respected by his peers and men, was killed. Lincoln's army retired slowly back to Charles Town and was joined by Moultrie's force that failed to land on John's Island because of a lack of rafts and boats. Lincoln lost 34 killed and 113 wounded, whereas Maitland suffered 26 killed and 103 wounded.

Several days following the battle, Maitland evacuated his position at Stono Ferry and rejoined the main army on John's Island. On June 26, the army crossed to Simmon's Island and then to Edisto Island with Maitland's men bringing up the rear. Following three days of rest, General Prevost and the main army crossed the St Heland Sound and arrived on Port Royal Island. Maitland's force, using the ferries and boats sent by General Prevost, sailed southward along the coast to rejoin General Prevost's force at Beaufort, South Carolina on July 8. Prevost left Maitland with a force of 800 on Port Royal Island and departed for Savannah with the main army.

As the British retired southward, General Lincoln was facing the reduction of his army as enlistments of many North Carolina and Virginia militiamen expired and they went home. Moreover, Lincoln was having difficulty filling the ranks of his six South Carolina Continental line regiments and requested a draft. To Lincoln's disappointment, but not surprise, the South Carolina Assembly rejected the request. It preferred the ranks to be filled with volunteers and not by conscripts. South Carolinians, Lincoln realized, were not very fond of a long-term Continental enlistment and of being subject to articles of war. These and other manpower shortages in the south led Congress to petition both Georgia and South Carolina to raise 3,000 slaves and enlist them into the armed forces. Both states fought the idea because of slave-owner complaints about compensation, among many other concerns. However a few slaves did join the ranks and eventually gained their freedom.

General Lincoln was also frustrated with the Continental Congress, and its apparent disinterest toward his Southern Department's concerns and issues. Although some help arrived in July, from a Light Dragoon regiment under Major John Jameson and a detachment of 400 Virginia troops under Colonel Richard Parker, there were not enough to attack the British in Savannah. To sustain his beleaguered force, Lincoln authorized the export of 1,500 barrels of rice to Martinique for the purchase of military stores unavailable on the continent. In addition to lacking just about everything necessary to keep an army in the field, Lincoln wrote to Rutledge about the need to prepare the Charles Town defenses and the deplorable condition of Fort Moultrie. He was convinced that unless conditions changed a determined

President Andrew Jackson's older brother, Hugh, died of heatstroke after the battle of Stono Ferry. Andrew and his other brother, Robert, were captured in 1781 fighting against the British. Robert died later that year from smallpox. (Library of Congress)

British attack would surely capture the capital. Adding to Lincoln's recruiting and retention problems, all troops from both armies had to deal with the oppressive heat. Moultrie wrote of the daily summer temperatures as 98 to 100 degrees in the shade. Although the militia and the Continental troops were accustomed to the heat, the men of the 71st Regiment, Hessian battalions, and Loyalists from New York and New Jersey found the humidity oppressive as it made their clothes stick to them, especially after violent thunderstorms. They also had to deal with swarms of sand flies, gnats, and mosquitoes that thrived in the marsh areas throughout the coastal region.

A bright spot for Lincoln came in the name of French Colonel Charles-François Sevelinges, Marquis de Brétigny, stationed in Charles Town, a former captain of musketeers to King Louis XVI. De Brétigny in support of the South Carolina assembly wrote to d'Estaing in the Caribbean, strongly urging him to support the southern cause to evict the British forces from Savannah. In his letter, de Brétigny wrote, "without firing a shot [*sans coup férir*] d'Estaing could win the victory." On July 17, 1779, he wrote his final request, "Never was this country in more need of succor. It is necessary to defend it against its enemies and against itself. All is lamentable confusion, few regular troops, no assistance from the North, a feeble and ill-disciplined militia, and a great lack of harmony among the leaders." D'Estaing finally accepted the offer and ordered his fleet to prepare to sail to Georgia.

Thomas Heyward Jr, South Carolina militia captain and signatory of the Declaration of Independence. He was wounded at the February 3, 1779 battle on Port Royal Island. (State Archives of Florida)

As Lincoln pleaded for more troops and supplies from the southern governors and Continental Congress, the British troops went into summer encampment at Beaufort and Savannah to await cooler temperatures before starting an active campaign in the autumn. In late July, Royal Governor Wright returned from England onboard HMS *Experiment* and quickly resumed office in Savannah as the royal governor of Georgia. He soon wrote to Lord Germain on July 31, "I shall look with utmost Anxiety and Impatience for more Troops from New York and hope they will be in our Neighborhood early in October, for till then, as our Troops that were here are so much Scattered about, I shall not Consider this Provence as safe." Earlier in the spring, Major-General Prevost had submitted his resignation letter to Lieutenant-General Clinton in New York asking to be relieved of duty on account of his health. Clinton approved his request and ordered Brigadier-General George Garth as his replacement and embarked on the *Experiment* for its return trip to Savannah.

THE FRENCH ARRIVE

On September 4, General Prevost received word of the sighting of five French ships sailing north off Tybee Island. Prevost's fear of a French intervention was confirmed by this sighting and he sent word to his outlying garrisons to make preparations for their return to Savannah. These detachments included Lieutenant-Colonel John Cruger's detachment of 100 Loyalist troops from DeLancy's 1st Battalion at Sunbury and Lieutenant-Colonel Maitland's

The French arrive

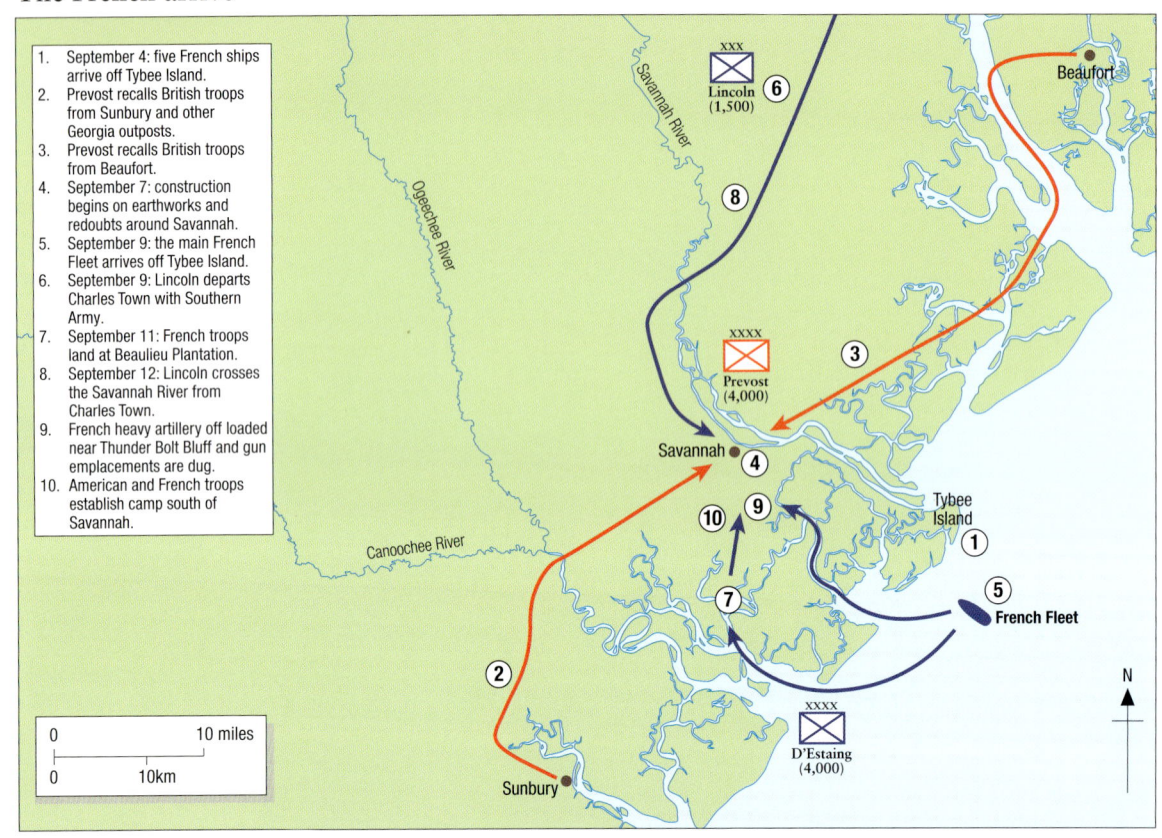

1. September 4: five French ships arrive off Tybee Island.
2. Prevost recalls British troops from Sunbury and other Georgia outposts.
3. Prevost recalls British troops from Beaufort.
4. September 7: construction begins on earthworks and redoubts around Savannah.
5. September 9: the main French Fleet arrives off Tybee Island.
6. September 9: Lincoln departs Charles Town with Southern Army.
7. September 11: French troops land at Beaulieu Plantation.
8. September 12: Lincoln crosses the Savannah River from Charles Town.
9. French heavy artillery off loaded near Thunder Bolt Bluff and gun emplacements are dug.
10. American and French troops establish camp south of Savannah.

800-man force at Beaufort on Port Royal Island, South Carolina. The ships that were sighted had been dispatched by d'Estaing with his Adjutant General (Viscount François de Fontanges) to confer with General Lincoln at Charles Town. Once the ships arrived, an agreement was quickly reached between the allied partners for the removal of British forces in Savannah. The Americans were to show cooperation in this new alliance and send several ships and boats to assist in the landing of French troops, cannons, and provide lumber for repairs and supplies for the French ships. D'Estaing's fleet had been operating successfully in the Caribbean, but needed those supplies to sustain itself off the Georgia coast in support of the upcoming operation. After agreeing to the Savannah plan, Lincoln sent his aide Major Thomas Pinckney and Captain Thomas Gadsden, 1st South Carolina Continental Regiment and younger brother to Christopher, with the Viscount de Fontanges to foster a close liaison with d'Estaing's staff. In addition, Lieutenant-Colonel Joseph Habersham was sent by Lincoln to assist with the debarkation at the landing site. D'Estaing had made it clear to Lincoln's liaison officers that he would spend no more than ten days along the coast because of the French fleet's vulnerability to the seasonal hurricanes and potential threat of the British Navy, not to mention the poor health conditions of his sailors.

General Lincoln's headquarters at Charles Town during the first week of September became a flurry of activity now that a plan had been developed with his new ally. He made preparations for his force of 2,000 men to march south on September 9 and assigned General Moultrie as commander of

Charles Town defenses. Orders went out to the South Carolina Continental Regiments at Charles Town to prepare to march and General Huger was directed to detach parties to scour the Savannah River from Two Sisters (ferry) down to Gibbons (Whitehall Plantation) to "collect all boats of every kind which may be in the river." The South Carolina militia units were called up by Governor Rutledge to proceed to Charles Town. Lincoln requested Rutledge keep several militia units in Charles Town "to hold themselves in readiness to march at a moment's warning." At this time, Lieutenant-Colonel Cruger's Loyalists departed Sunbury and Lincoln received an urgent letter from Georgia Colonel Walton, the senior American officer held by parole in Sunbury, requesting a force be sent to protect the American officers held prisoner there. He and his fellow prisoners were extremely worried about the violence that would result from the unruly Loyalist groups that were sure to enter Sunbury when they discovered Cruger had departed. The Georgia officers included Colonel John Stirk (3rd Regiment), Captain Thomas Morris (2nd Regiment) and Major John Habersham (1st Regiment), younger brother to Lieutenant-Colonel Joseph Habersham, who had signed their oaths earlier in the year and were waiting to be exchanged for British officers. The oath they signed read, "Oath of the Sunbury prisoners of war to their captors, promising they will not leave Sunbury or allow anyone to free them before they are legally exchanged. If they are freed, they will attempt to return to their captors; if return is impossible, the prisoners swear not to take up arms against King George until they are legally exchanged." Upon receipt of Walton's request, Lincoln dispatched 25 men to Sunbury to protect these officers.

On September 7, there were 20 French ships sighted and two days later 52 ships were sighted off Tybee Island. The sighting of these French ships off the Georgia coast during that time of year astonished Prevost and his officers because of potential storms and hurricanes. He sent riders with orders for Maitland and Cruger and other smaller detachments to

On the stormy evening of September 11, 1779, a force of 1,200 French troops began disembarking from French frigates into longboats on the Vernon River and came ashore at the Beaulieu Plantation 12 miles south of Savannah. (Drawing by Bernard Harris)

Plaque dedication to the French infantry landings at the Beaulieu Plantation. Unlike the French landings in Newport, Rhode Island the previous year, d'Estaing was determined to engage the British Army. (Daughters of the American Revolution)

reinforce his 1,500-man army at Savannah. Prevost ordered his chief engineer, Captain Moncrief, to construct a fortification line protecting Savannah from a land assault. To start, Moncrief had only four dilapidated redoubts (earthen fortifications) surrounding the city which he could build upon for his design of a defense in depth. Since the British capture of Savannah, no significant effort had been made to improve existing redoubts or build any defensive positions. Moncrief estimated he would need additional manpower to build the fortification to help augment the working parties of British, Hessian, and Loyalist soldiers. The British Army, unlike its colonial counterparts, quickly paid its Loyalist slave masters for the right to hire their slaves, rather than resort to impressment. With Royal Governor Wright's approval, Moncrief gathered over 250 slaves from the nearby rice plantations, 59 black pioneers, and 218 black volunteers to serve the King and get paid for their service. One of the first tasks he had for them was to expand the old Savannah fort (renamed Fort Prevost) on the east side of the city along the river. In addition, houses at the outskirts of town were dismantled, one of which was Wright's plantation, in order to build firing platforms and to clear a line of cannon fire several hundred yards in front of the fortifications. In this open field he had a thick ring of abatis installed to impede an attacker's cohesion. Fifty yards behind the abatis were a series of redoubts and entrenchments, which included sand. By including sand in the redoubts and entrenchments, any possible damage caused by cannonballs could easily be repaired and would minimize casualties to the defenders. The Americans had used sand in their defensive works at Fort Sullivan. The four existing redoubts were reinforced and ten new ones were constructed, giving the British a total of 14, stretching in a vast semicircle around Savannah from east, south, and west, anchored by the Savannah River to the north. The redoubts had high earthen walls surrounded on three and a half sides by a deep ditch with abatis sticking straight up from the bottom of the ditch. At the back of the redoubt was an entrance. Each of the redoubts was flanked by artillery batteries. These batteries contained a total of 76 cannons of various sizes – 18lb, 9lb, to 6lb. Many of the cannons were taken off the British ships anchored in Savannah's harbor and manned by their sailors. Behind the redoubts, 50 to 100 yards back, was a line of earthworks for the forces held in reserve.

In order to meet the expectation of the allied effort, General Lincoln organized his army of 2,000, consisting of Continentals and militia, and marched for Savannah. Lincoln's force arrived on the north bank of the Savannah River at Zubley's Ferry on September 11, but then had to find ferries and any other floating device to transport his army, cannons and supplies across the river, since General Huger's force had not arrived yet. Enroute Lincoln had parties repair the bridges previously destroyed in May. Lincoln's advance parties were able to locate only one canoe for the crossing, since the ferries and boats were either destroyed or taken by the British during their expedition in April. By the morning of the 12th, Lincoln's force, along with Pulaski's cavalry, began crossing the Savannah River and, by September 14, they had finally crossed it, along with their cannons and supply wagons. Although, Prevost did not send a force to challenge Lincoln's crossing, the passage across the river was very slow on account of the marshland on either side of the river and the few watercraft available. In addition to Huger's delay, Brigadier-General McIntosh had been sent orders to depart Augusta with his force and obtain all watercraft for the river crossing while enroute to Zubley's Ferry, but his force did not arrive until after Lincoln's force crossed at the ferry site. While his army struggled across the river, Lincoln had had no communications with the French since their last meeting in Charles Town, and could only hope they were honoring their end of the agreement to capture Savannah. At the time of Lincoln's army crossing the Savannah River, the French navy sealed off Savannah from the Atlantic, and in a brief engagement off the South Carolina coast the 32-gun French ship *l'Amazon* defeated the 20-gun British frigate HMS *Ariel*.

As Lincoln was assembling his force in Charles Town, d'Estaing had met with Major Pinckney onboard his flagship the frigate *Languedoc* and agreed with his recommendation for the landing site at Beaulieu Plantation some 12 miles south of the Savannah River entrance. To ensure British ships were contained on the Savannah River, d'Estaing decided to capture the small fort on Tybee Island and maintain a naval presence near the mouth of the river. On the afternoon of September 9, longboats were assembled alongside the *Languedoc* off Tybee Island with several hundred French infantry and were slowly rowed toward the island. D'Estaing, Major Pinckney and about 20 of his staff and soldiers came ashore ahead of the lumbering longboats rowing against strong offshore currents. Having arrived on the beach ahead of his troops, Pinckney observed an argument between d'Estaing and his Adjutant General, Viscount de Fontanges, about landing the 700 men in the longboats to assault the British fort on the island. In an apparent breakdown in communication the landing parties never received orders to land, nor were they instructed that their objective was to attack a fort. Near the beach several members of d'Estaing's staff and Pinckney questioned two local

A replica of the Spring Hill redoubt (about a third of actual size) as seen from the attacking French and American soldiers' perspective. (Photograph by Bernard Harris)

slaves, who indicated the British troops on the island had recently departed with their two cannons and had destroyed the small fort. As the winds picked up in intensity, only 200 French soldiers were able to land on Tybee Island and the remaining 500 men were forced to spend the night in their crowded longboats until the winds subsided the following morning. The next day was spent loading the 700, minus a small detachment left on Tybee Island, back on their ships and sailing south to the Ossaba Sound for their landing at Beaulieu Plantation along the Vernon River. The incident and the apparent lack of concern d'Estaing demonstrated for his men spread throughout the fleet.

D'Estaing's fleet arrived off the Ossaba Sound on the morning of September 11, but many of his ships were having difficulty getting over the sandbar because of the winds and current. Around mid-afternoon, d'Estaing ordered his troops onto longboats to follow the ship to their landing site. His plan was for the ships and longboats to enter the Vernon River together for protection, in case the landing was to be opposed by the British. On account of the adverse weather conditions, it was not until 10.00pm when the first boats carrying his 1,500 soldiers were able to land, but a large majority of his men were crowded into the longboats and spent a rainy night being rowed to the landing site. To add to their misery, his soldiers carried only three days' rations of food and water. It was not until late afternoon on September 12 that all 1,500 troops and d'Estaing along with his staff were finally able to land at the Beaulieu Plantation site. D'Estaing had turned command of the fleet over to Count de Broyes, while he conducted operations against Savannah. D'Estaing and these troops would suffer through the stormy weather without adequate shelter and food for the next several days, because the storms had forced his ships farther out to sea. It was not until the weather cleared on the 16th, that the French were able to land the rest of their 2,500 troops. As with Lincoln's crossing, General Prevost made no attempt to delay or challenge the French landings or delay their advance toward Savannah; instead his efforts focused on fortifying his positions around Savannah.

Several days later General Lincoln's lead elements began to arrive, composed of 1,500 Continentals and militia, and established a camp to the left (west) of General de Noailles's French division. On September 16, the French had 2,400 troops on the march from Beaulieu Plantation and were strung out for 3 miles from Savannah. Advancing at the head of 150 grenadiers to within a mile of the city, Count d'Estaing sent a flag of truce with a summons for General Prevost. D'Estaing, confident of victory and unbeknownst to Lincoln, requested the surrender of the British garrison: "to the arms of the King of France." The summons did not mention the Americans, which infuriated Lincoln, who found out about the summons only later that day; this added to the friction between the commanders and their armies. To bide more time, and in anticipation of the arrival of Maitland's force, Prevost requested and received a 24-hour truce. To sum up the American disbelief, Lieutenant-Colonel Francis Marion, commander of the 2nd South Carolina Continental regiment, later to earn fame as the Swamp Fox, spoke for many of his fellow officers in their frustration, "My God! Who ever heard of anything like this before? First allow an enemy to entrench and then fight him!" In a breach of European protocol, Prevost continued to build his fortifications and was reinforced at the most opportune moment by half of Maitland's force. As Lincoln and d'Estaing toured their lines during the truce,

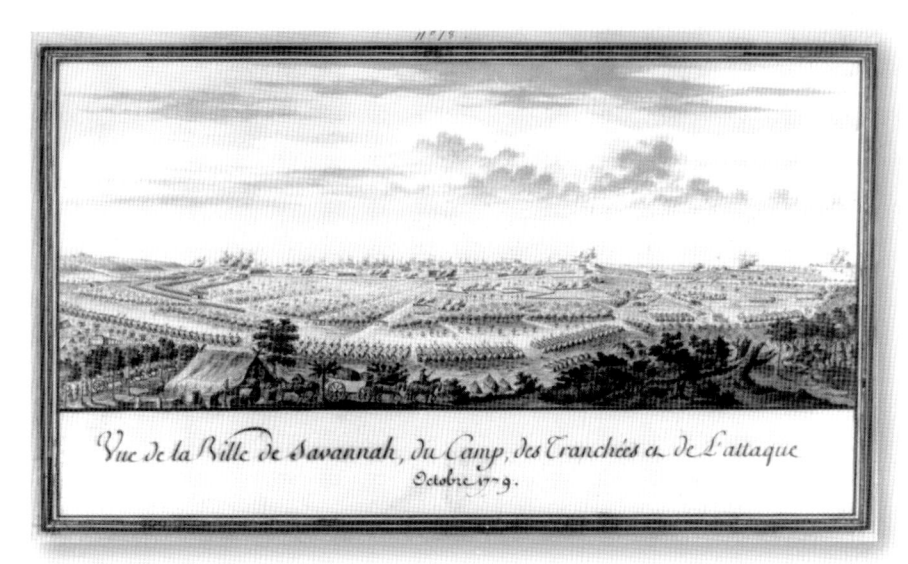

Vue de la Ville de Savannah, du Camp, des Tranchées et de L'attaque Octobre 1779.

The French camp was located to the southeast of Savannah, whereas the American camp was situated southwest of the city. To alleviate friction and animosity between the two armies, special passes were required to enter either camp. (Library of Congress)

they stopped on Brewton Hill and witnessed Maitland's men rowing upriver to the city and realized their quick victory over the British garrison had just slipped away. D'Estaing then looked over to see Lincoln fall sound asleep.

Upon receiving the orders from General Prevost to return to Savannah, Maitland made an epic trek from Beaumont with his 800-man force. His men sailed and rowed behind Hilton Head Island to avoid French ships stationed at the mouth of the Broad River and entered Calibogue Sound. As they neared the Savannah River, they could see the French ships lying at anchor several miles downriver from Savannah and learned from local black fishermen that they could follow Wall's Cut, a little-known passage behind Daufuskie Island. Dragging and pulling their heavy boats through miles of deep mud and shallow winding salt creeks, they reached the river about 3 miles downstream of Savannah. A Loyalist in Savannah wrote about the effect she saw upon Maitland's arrival, "Our men … suffered from fatigue and want of rest, but in the height of our despondence [Lieutenant] Colonel Maitland effected a junction in a wonderful manner … thus giving new life and joy to the worn-out troops."

During General Prevost's council of war with his commanders to determine d'Estaing's offer, Maitland was emphatic they would defend Savannah and not even contemplate surrendering the city. On September 17, Prevost's written response to d'Estaing stated,

> SIR:- In answer to the letter of your Excellency, which I had the honour to receive about twelve last night, I am to acquaint you that having laid the whole correspondence before the King's civil Governor, and military officers of rank assembled in Council of War, the unanimous determination has been, that though we cannot look upon our post as absolutely inexpungable, yet that it may and ought to be defended: therefore, the evening gun to be fired this evening at an hour before sundown, shall be the signal for recommencing hostilities …

American and French officers soon accused each other of neglect for allowing Maitland's force to depart Beaufort unscathed. In addition to this episode and based on French officer accounts, they did not feel American officers or soldiers were of the same quality as their army. This friction was one of the main reasons the French and American camps were separated. In addition, commanders issued orders for their troops not to enter their allied camps without permission, in order to prevent fights from breaking out between them.

D'Estaing realized his promise of a ten-day operation would not be met as they agreed a siege would be necessary and began to work on digging trenches during a torrential rainstorm. The violent storm forced Count de Broyes to order the fleet to get under way and move farther out to sea to avoid the risk of a ship running aground. On September 20, to protect the river approaches to Savannah, the British sank two unseaworthy ships, *Rose* and *Savannah*, in the channel to prevent the larger French deep-draft ships and American vessels from moving upriver to the city. Furthermore, to counter the threat from the river, Captain Moncrief fashioned fire rafts to discourage the approach of enemy ships if they were to move closer to Savannah and even managed to have a boom of chains erected across the river just west of the city, protected by the frigate HMS *Germaine*. As the rains subsided at midday on September 22, the French began to offload their large-caliber cannons, to include shipboard cannons and mortars, at their new base near Thunderbolt Bluff on the St Augustine Creek, just 6 miles from Savannah. That evening they dug trenches along with firing positions directly opposite the British center position, under the supervision of French engineer, Captain Antoine O'Connor. Although a lack of digging tools proved a handicap, French and American soldiers built the trenches to within 300 yards of the British lines. In addition to the challenges of digging trenches, the French had experienced great difficulty transporting their cannons and mortars because of the muddy roads and limited number of horses and draft animals available. Eventually the batteries were dug and cannons were emplaced. The battery on the allied left was composed of six 18-pounders and an equal number of 12-pounders. On the right, a second battery of five 18-pounders and seven 12-pounders was erected. Behind the trenches another French battery of nine mortars was established. The Americans established a battery of four 6-pounders, representing their entire artillery strength.

Capture of HMS *Experiment* off Hilton Head, South Carolina on September 24, 1779. Captain Wallace after departing New York City was unaware of the strong French naval presence off the Georgia–Carolina coast. (Drawing by Bernard Harris)

SIEGE

The siege of Savannah began on September 23. As the French infantry and marines continued to transport their artillery and dig trenches toward the British southern defensive position, the crews on the French ships were suffering from scurvy and lack of fresh water. The salted beef and pork they were eating greatly contributed to their thirst for fresh water and the bread on hand, which had been in barrels for two years, had decayed and was full of worms. The feeling throughout the fleet was of abandonment by d'Estaing, who they believed had invested all his attention toward the army. Unbeknownst to many of his ships' captains, d'Estaing's concern for his crews in unpredictable hurricane conditions was the driving factor for his ten-day timeline to capture Savannah. Although conditions were deteriorating for the French crews, they were still an effective force.

On Friday, September 24, en route to Savannah from New York City, the HMS *Experiment* (50 guns) and two supply ships were damaged in a gale off the coast of Hilton Head, South Carolina. The French naval reports of this action noted: "*Experiment*, commanded by Captain Sir James Wallace, lost its masts and bowsprit in a gale and became stranded." Three French ships were dispatched to find the *Experiment* and the two supply ships, *Cartel Champion* and *Myrtle*, it was escorting. By 8.00pm, two French warships closed with the *Experiment*. The French 54-gun ship *Sagittaire*, commanded by Captain d'Albert de Rions, fired two broadsides at the *Experiment* to start the engagement. After exchanging a number of shots, the mast of the *Experiment* was shot off, which forced *Experiment* to surrender, along with the two supply ships. The supply ships were loaded with 700lb of rations and pay for the Savannah defenders. However, the biggest catch onboard *Experiment* was Prevost's replacement, General Garth.

Meanwhile earlier that day, British Major Graham led an early morning sortie around 7.00am to disrupt the digging by French and American soldiers. Three light infantry companies consisting of 97 men were to disrupt the work on the siege lines and entice the French to launch an assault. The British in this surprise sortie suffered 21 casualties compared with the French loss of 70. The sortie marked the first fight on land between British and French soldiers during the war. The French did not pursue the British but continued with their siege works. As the digging continued, the British launched a second sortie on the evening of September 27, led by Major Archibald McArthur, consisting of a detachment from the 71st. As the firing started, French troops quickly responded and advanced to McArthur's left while a number of Americans advanced on his right flank. In the darkness, McArthur's men quickly withdrew to their positions, and in the ensuing confusion the French and American parties fired upon each other. Several soldiers were killed and wounded until they realized they were firing upon one another. By October 2, Captain Moncrief had completed a 15-gun battery near the large barracks located in the British center facing south, to counter the French siege guns.

Three companies of the British 16th Light Infantry sortied against the French as they dug their siege lines. Although it was a temporary disruption, the French had to increase the number of soldiers in the siege area to guard against future sorties. (Anness Publishing Ltd)

BOMBARDMENT

The next day, October 3, French cannons, mortars, and fire from the French ships began the bombardment of British fortified positions around Savannah. The firing of 33 cannons and nine mortars in the siege works continued for five days and caused more damage to the city inhabitants than to the British-held entrenchments and redoubts. Although one soldier was killed, 40 residents and slaves died during this period, a number of whom were women and children. Anthony Stokes, chief justice in Savannah, noted during the bombardment, "there was hardly a house which had not been shot through and some of them were almost destroyed." Another citizen in Savannah described the effect: "hardly one of the four hundred and fifty dwellings in town had not been shot through." General Prevost's wife, Anne, wrote of her experience during the bombardment:

> I had scarcely finished writing before I heard a frightful noise. It is the fall of a bomb which has shaken the weak edifice in which we are, crushed the neighboring house, and set on fire the casks of spirituous liquors. I was not recovered from the impression before they came to tell me I must quit my asylum and the neighborhood of a house on fire. Dragged by the Captain, who took my son in his arms, I took my daughter in mine. I went out of the cellar and trembling traversed part of the town. We escaped at last the danger of the fire, but our flight exposed us to that of the cannon's bombs.

The Bombardment of Savannah, 1,000 shells fired over four days from French and American cannons and mortars. French ships downriver also fired on the British defenses, but many of their shots fell short and damaged a number of houses in the city. (Library of Congress)

By the third night of the bombardment, several residents, both white and black, along with some soldiers' families, fled to the village of Yamacraw, immediately west of Savannah. From there, the women and children then sought safety across the river to Hutchinson Island where they hid in a large rice barn. To provide them with protection, Prevost sent a company of Cherokee Native Americans and a company of armed slaves serving in the South Carolina militia to the island. Governor Wright and many of the officers' wives took refuge with their husbands in their defensive positions, when it became clear they were the safest places to hide during the bombardment. On October 6, General Prevost sent out a request that the women and children be allowed to leave Savannah for their safety, but it was rejected by Lincoln. They had endured the bombing of more than 1,000 shells on the city. A few critics claim Lincoln denied the request, since Prevost had denied an earlier request for Brigadier-General McIntosh's wife to leave Savannah. Lincoln also believed that the arduous living conditions of the civilians while enduring the bombardment might influence Prevost to surrender.

The next day, Thursday, October 7, the French began to fire incendiary bombs into the town. One American in camp wrote to his wife about witnessing the incendiary attack, "the whole [city] will be in flames by nightfall." On account of the efforts of the residents and soldiers, coupled with the previous day's rain, only several houses were burned. Later that day, d'Estaing called a council

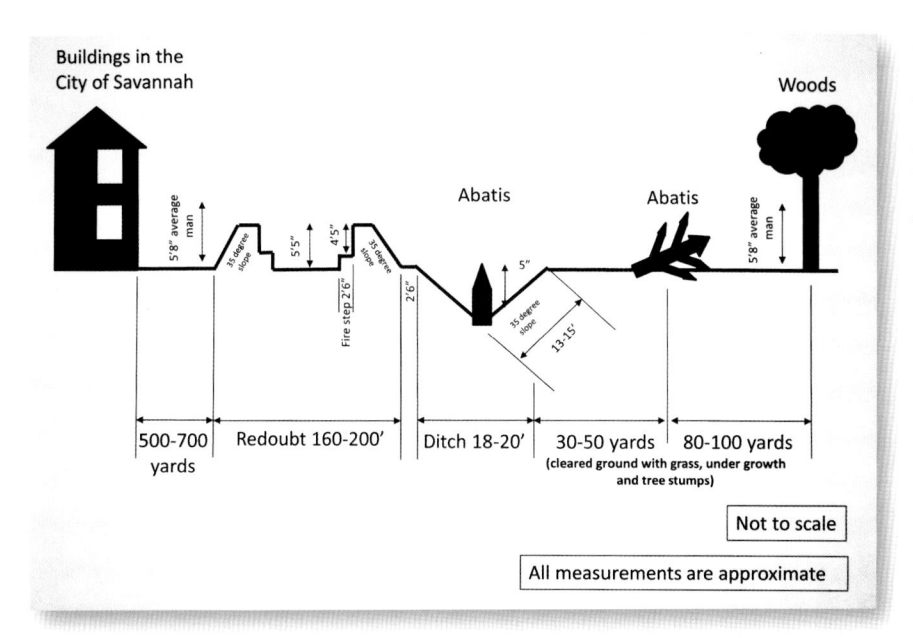

A cross section of the Spring Hill redoubt defense with approximate distances between obstacles. American and French troops had to overcome these obstacles to reach the British and loyalist troops defending the redoubt. (Diagram by Bernard Harris)

of war with Lincoln and their senior officers to discuss the situation. The admiral's chief engineer, Antoine O'Connor, informed him that he would need ten more days of digging to penetrate the British earthworks. D'Estaing, fully aware that he had surpassed his commitment to his fleet, knew he did not have that time and informed Lincoln they must either raise the siege or attack. Moreover, he knew his sailors were suffering on their ships from lack of food and water and there were reports that 35 sailors were dying per day.

The evening of October 8, d'Estaing assembled his senior officers again along with Lincoln, and his officers proposed a plan to attack the next day. D'Estaing informed them he planned for an early-morning assault at 4.00am on Saturday, October 9. Many of the French officers, including his Adjutant General, Viscount de Fontanges, along with Lincoln attempted to dissuade him from conducting a frontal assault. They believed their forces were not strong enough to conduct a frontal assault on the British fortified positions and needed more time to continue advancing their siege works to the British line. D'Estaing rebutted their protests by boasting "extreme bravery can conquer everything." He went on to announce, "I will march at the head and you will follow me." The attack was focused on the British right flank at a point where the swampy rice fields joined their fortified line. The morning prior, Major Pierre Charles L'Enfant, an officer in John Laurens' elite corps of light infantry, led five volunteers to clear away the abatis constructed about 50 yards in front of the Spring Hill redoubt outer defensive ring. They attempted to kindle the abatis, but the damp green wood failed to burn. (L'Enfant would later achieve fame as the architect of Washington, DC.) D'Estaing's plan called for a total of five columns, three French and two American, to attack points along and adjacent to the Spring Hill redoubt on the British right flank. A fourth French column would be held as a reserve. The timing of the allied attack, 4.00am, was crucial to success. However, based on d'Estaing's plan, two of the French columns would be composed of his various regiments' grenadier and light infantry (chasseur) troops. Even though time was critical, the French had to reorganize their forces that night, and march from their camps, passing through the American camps to their start line; carrying this out at night only added to the confusion and loss of time. Furthermore, guides for the French columns got lost in the dense, pre-dawn fog and delayed their arrival to the positions of attack. D'Estaing's plan called for four French columns (divisions) consisting of a vanguard, a right column, a left column, and a reserve.

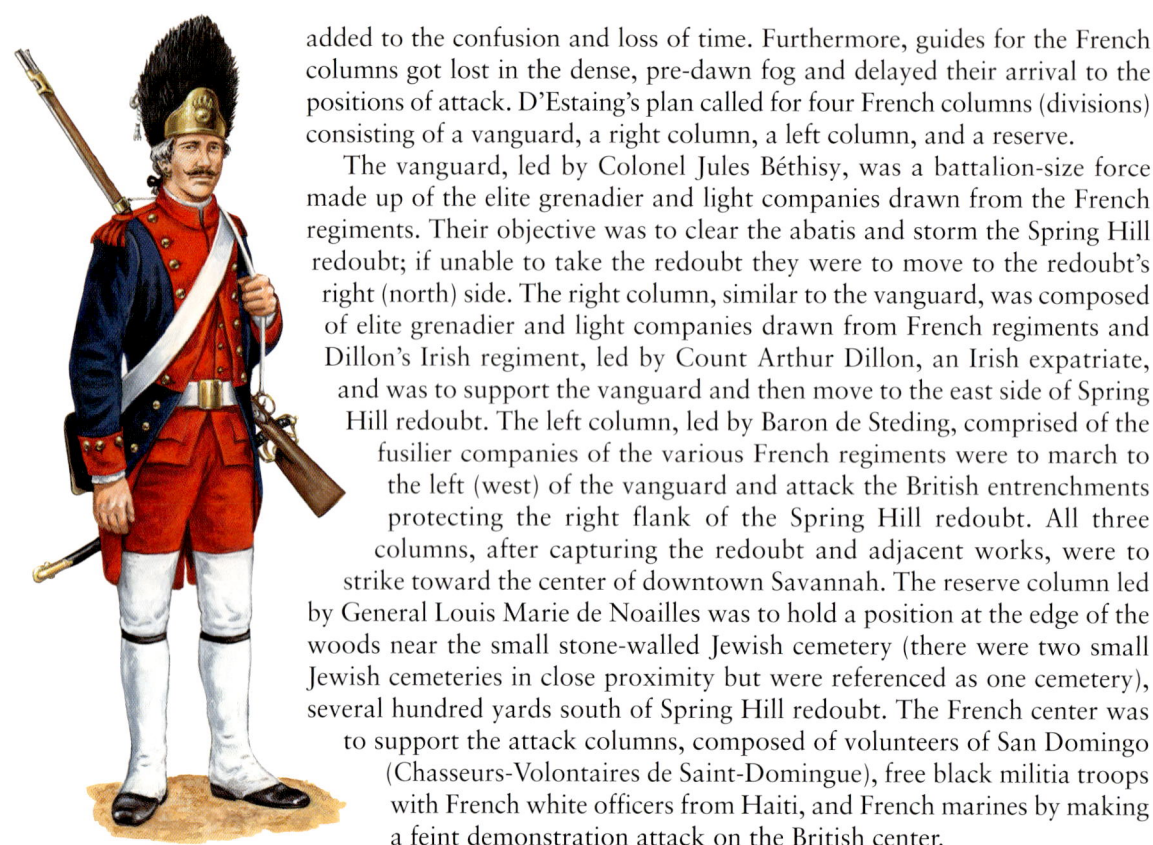

The vanguard, led by Colonel Jules Béthisy, was a battalion-size force made up of the elite grenadier and light companies drawn from the French regiments. Their objective was to clear the abatis and storm the Spring Hill redoubt; if unable to take the redoubt they were to move to the redoubt's right (north) side. The right column, similar to the vanguard, was composed of elite grenadier and light companies drawn from French regiments and Dillon's Irish regiment, led by Count Arthur Dillon, an Irish expatriate, and was to support the vanguard and then move to the east side of Spring Hill redoubt. The left column, led by Baron de Steding, comprised of the fusilier companies of the various French regiments were to march to the left (west) of the vanguard and attack the British entrenchments protecting the right flank of the Spring Hill redoubt. All three columns, after capturing the redoubt and adjacent works, were to strike toward the center of downtown Savannah. The reserve column led by General Louis Marie de Noailles was to hold a position at the edge of the woods near the small stone-walled Jewish cemetery (there were two small Jewish cemeteries in close proximity but were referenced as one cemetery), several hundred yards south of Spring Hill redoubt. The French center was to support the attack columns, composed of volunteers of San Domingo (Chasseurs-Volontaires de Saint-Domingue), free black militia troops with French white officers from Haiti, and French marines by making a feint demonstration attack on the British center.

Lincoln's two American columns were to march behind the French columns and attack the British Carolina redoubt just north of the Spring Hill redoubt. Furthermore, in addition to the feint in the center, General Huger was to lead a feint against the British left flank. Following d'Estaing's council of war, Lincoln issued the following orders that night to his forces and sent a copy to General Moultrie in Charles Town which read:

> The Watch word to be used was "Lewis" to prevent friendly fire as both his forces and French units assembled into the columns of attack and marched in the early morning hours to the assault positions. The soldiers will be immediately supplied with 40 rounds of cartridges; a spare flint; and have their arms in good order. The whole parade at 1 o'clock [1.00am]. The guards of the camp, will be formed of the invalids, and charged to keep the fires as usual, in camp. The column will move to the left of the French troops, taking care not to interfere with them. The troops will carry on their hats, a piece of white paper to be recognized.

Lincoln's right column, led by Lieutenant-Colonel John Laurens, consisted of the American light troops and other hand-picked units. Pulaski's cavalry brigade was to be the vanguard for the American right column and exploit any opening found. The left column, led by Brigadier-General Lachlan McIntosh, consisted of three South Carolina Continental regiments and was the far left column of attack. Huger's attack was to be carried out by 500 men, his additional troops were assigned to the French center to protect the French battery siege lines.

French bombardiers and sailors manned the siege cannons used against the British defenses in Savannah. (Anness Publishing Ltd)

The British defenses on October 9 were as follows. The left flank was defended by the 1st Battalion 71st Regiment, the von Trumbach Regiment, and DeLancy's 2nd Battalion. The center was held by New York loyalist battalions and the von Wissenbach Regiment led by Colonel von Porbeck. The Spring Hill redoubt was under the command of Captain Tawes and defended by 110 troops consisting of his dragoons (28 men), 4th Battalion from the 60th Regiment (28 men), and South Carolina Loyalists (54 men). To the right (north) of Spring Hill redoubt was the Carolina redoubt consisting of 90 North Carolina Loyalists (survivors from Kettle Creek) under Colonel Hamilton, along with 75 Georgia Loyalists. At the far right flank (western approach) was the Ebenezer Battery consisting of 31 marines under the command of Captains Manly and Stiel. General Prevost was fully aware his weak point was along his center position. That had been the focus of the French bombardment, so he placed the 2nd Battalion, 71st Regiment in reserve behind it. The right flank reserve consisted of three grenadier companies of the 16th, one company of Royal Marines, and the 71st Light Infantry.

A replica of the abatis that were dug into the Spring Hill redoubt. The obstacles were designed to disrupt the cohesion of an attacking force. (Photograph by Scott Martin)

ATTACK ON THE SPRING HILL REDOUBT

The assault scheduled for 4.00am did not commence until 5.30am, when the dawn's early morning light started to reveal the open fields in front of the British fortified positions. The British were up and ready, since there were accounts the 71st Regiment's bagpipes played their tunes; however other reports suggest a deserter from the Charles Town Grenadiers informed the British of the impending attack. Nevertheless, alert British sentinels detected the assault columns and gave the warning; d'Estaing, hearing firing from the British far left, against Huger's attack, and, not waiting for all the assault columns to get into position, placed himself at the head of his vanguard column and ordered it to advance at the double quick. He shouted "Vive le Roi" as it charged the 200 yards from the wood line to the redoubt. The three British gun batteries on either side of Spring Hill redoubt, each with five to six cannons, began to fire grapeshot at the onrushing French troops. Through the hail of grapeshot and mounting casualties the grenadiers and light troops continued to rush forward and hack their way through the abatis with handheld axes some 50 yards from the redoubt. D'Estaing, wounded in the arm, urged his men forward. The French and American troops had orders not to shoot until the Spring Hill redoubt was taken. That was a lesson Lincoln conveyed to d'Estaing after his troops hesitated and traded volley fire with an entrenched enemy, rather than continue their charge on the British at the battle of Stono Ferry several months earlier.

As casualties started to mount, the two left assault columns struggled through the swampy ground and began shifting to their right toward the Spring Hill redoubt. Following the breakdown of the initial vanguard assault inspired by d'Estaing, Dillon's right column charged through the abatis and struck the Spring Hill redoubt northwestern front; several of the Irish (in their red jackets) reached the parapet berm and momentarily entered the redoubt initiating a furious melee with Captain Tawes' defenders. While leading the charge up the earthen wall, Major Brown of Dillon's regiment fell backward into the ditch. He was the senior French officer to die in the assault and his men repulsed at the berm huddled at the redoubt base with men from initial assault columns.

Meanwhile, Baron de Steding's left column, having advanced through a muddy swamp to the west of the Spring Hill and Carolina redoubts, started to break apart their formation. To complicate his column's movement further, the vanguard survivors that had retreated to their left ran into the column causing disruption and loss of momentum. As the troops intermingled they began to congregate on the only dry section of their advance in face of the Carolina redoubt on the road from Savannah to Augusta. To continue this forward movement meant advancing through more swampy rice fields, so commanders on the scene shifted the focus to the right and followed the road to the northwest side of the Spring Hill redoubt. Officers and senior enlisted troops began repeatedly to urge their men to advance along the road to the Spring Hill redoubt. Throughout this ordeal, each assault was beaten back and the mass of men suffered from the defenders' musket fire and grapeshot fired from emplaced cannons, as well as long-range solid shot fired by the British armed brig *Germaine* and two galleys on the river. During this time, d'Estaing was hit in the leg, his second wound during the attack, and his second in command, the Viscount de Fontanges, was also wounded, and desperately urged d'Estaing to order a retreat. Around this time, Laurens' column entered the fray. As the intermingled French assault columns attempted to regain control, Laurens on his own accord, shifted the advance of his column from the Carolina redoubt and moved to his right to attack the Spring Hill redoubt. Although the 1st Virginia Continentals fell behind, the 2nd South Carolina Continentals and Charles Town militia charged home. Laurens' advance covered dry ground from the wood line to the redoubt; as most of the fire was being directed on the mass of French soldiers in the ditch and directly in front of the two redoubts, most of Laurens' men were unscathed as they charged the last 50 yards. At the head of Laurens' column was the 2nd South Carolina Continental led by Lieutenant-Colonel Marion and its pair of silk flags (one red and the other blue) that had been presented to the regiment by Mrs. Bernard Elliott of Charles Town, as a reward from the ladies of the city for the regiment's heroic defense of Fort Sullivan in June 1776. Both flags were raised on the Spring Hill parapet as both color bearers were killed. Sergeant William Jasper in his final minutes handed the flag to Lieutenant John Bush who fell shortly afterward with the red flag under his body. The blue flag color bearer, was killed as well, but was placed on the berm by the wounded Sergeant McDonald, who carried back both flags when retreat was sounded. The impetus of the Laurens column carried a small number of Americans, French, and Irish up and over the parapet near the northern face of the redoubt. A short but fierce melee ensued as the attackers were thrown back again by the resolute defenders led by Captain Tawes, who personally killed three South Carolina Continentals near the redoubt entrance before he was killed. His steadfast determination kept his command intact as they repeatedly held their position against overwhelming numbers. After 45 minutes, the four assault columns co-mingled in the field in front of the redoubt and crowded in the narrow ditch to the northwestern and southwestern face of the redoubt, while suffering under British musket

Dr. James Lynah, chief surgeon of the South Carolina Light Dragoons, commented that Pulaski had remained conscious during the entire operation to remove the grapeshot (pictured), while displaying the utmost courage he had ever seen in a patient. (Georgia Historical Society)

and canister enfilade fire. After the battle, General Moultrie wrote in his journal from first-hand accounts: "our troops were so crowded in the ditch and upon the berm that they could hardly raise an arm, and while they were in this situation, huddled up together, the British loaded and fired deliberately into the packed masses."

In an attempt to ascertain the situation, and as casualties increased due to this inferno, Pulaski rode out from the tree line to find an opportunity for his cavalry to charge, in an attempt to get behind the redoubt as per d'Estaing's original orders. He soon fell from his horse when he was hit in his upper right thigh and groin by grapeshot fired from a cannon. He was quickly carried from the field by his men and was attended to by Dr. James Lynah, chief surgeon of the South Carolina Light Dragoons. A few additional cannon shots caused some of his cavalry to flee, causing some to ride through the retiring French and American soldiers.

Urged by his second in command and other officers, d'Estaing finally ordered a retreat. Around this time, Major Glazier, who had been held in reserve, led his grenadiers from the 16th Regiment and 60 Royal Marines with fixed bayonets and charged. They cleared the ramparts and redoubt ditch of the remaining American and French soldiers. In addition, Lieutenant-Colonel Maitland rushed over three companies of the 71st, but they arrived too late to support Glazier's counterattack. The impetus of his counterattack pushed the British past the redoubt and abatis in pursuit of the attackers until

Sergeant William Jasper monument in Savannah's Madison Square. Sergeant William Jasper, the hero of the June 28, 1776 bombardment of Fort Sullivan. During that British bombardment, the flagstaff was shot away. Sergeant Jasper shouted to Colonel Moultrie that they should not fight without a flag and promptly climbed the parapet under fire to place the flag on it. Jasper was later praised by John Rutledge, President of South Carolina (1776–78) and presented with a sword. He fell mortally wounded while saving his 2nd South Carolina Continental flag during the assault on the Spring Hill redoubt. (Library of Congress)

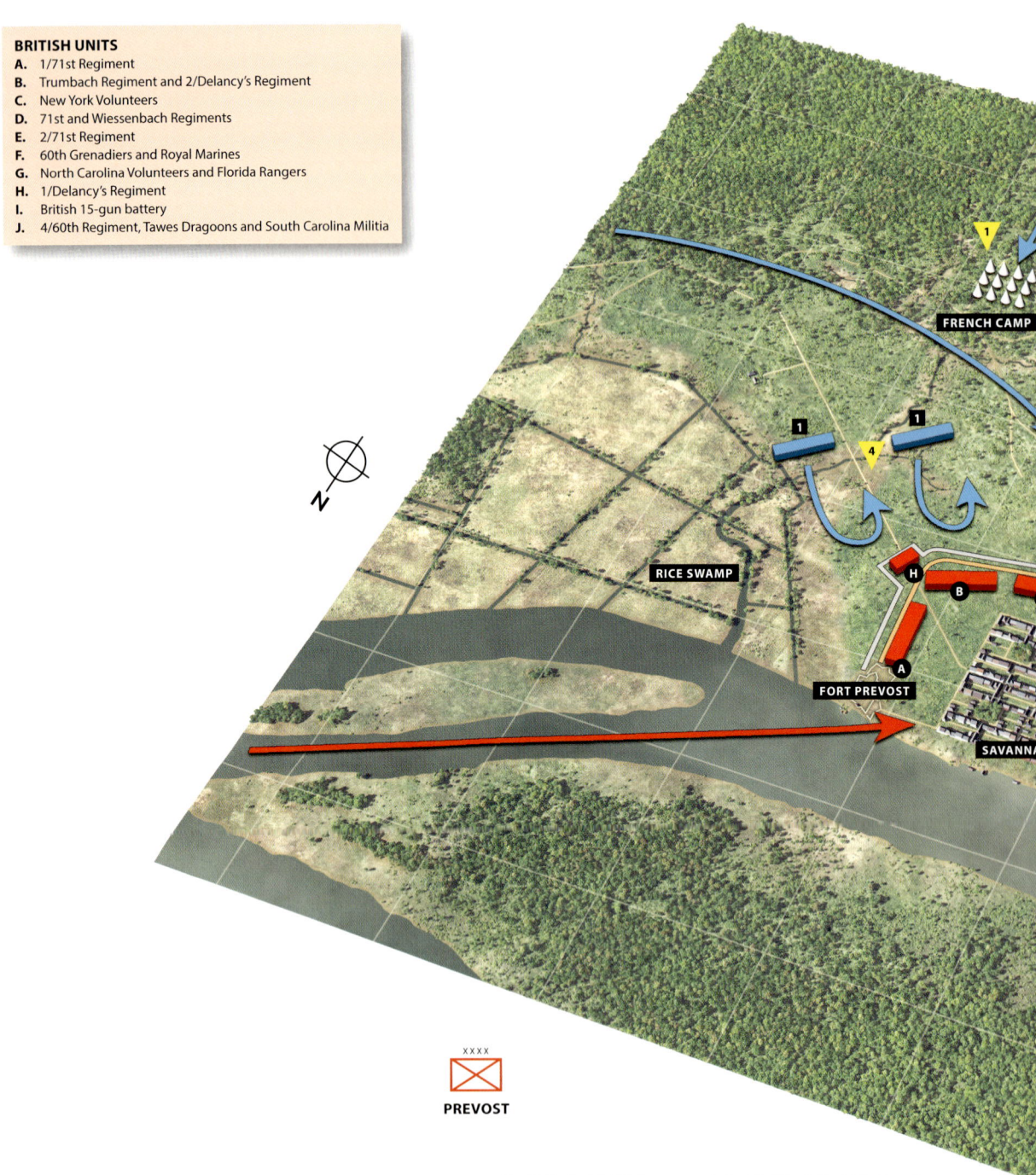

BRITISH UNITS
A. 1/71st Regiment
B. Trumbach Regiment and 2/Delancy's Regiment
C. New York Volunteers
D. 71st and Wiessenbach Regiments
E. 2/71st Regiment
F. 60th Grenadiers and Royal Marines
G. North Carolina Volunteers and Florida Rangers
H. 1/Delancy's Regiment
I. British 15-gun battery
J. 4/60th Regiment, Tawes Dragoons and South Carolina Militia

FRENCH CAMP

RICE SWAMP

FORT PREVOST

SAVANNA

PREVOST

EVENTS

1. After midnight the French columns assemble and march to the American camp.
2. The two American columns follow behind the French columns to the assembly point near the Jewish cemeteries.
3. Due to delays and getting lost in the woods, d'Estaing's Vanguard is the only column in their attack position around 5:30am.
4. Brigadier-General Huger's feint attack commences around 5:30am.
5. D'Estaing upon hearing the British fire against Huger's force, orders the attack on the Spring Hill redoubt before all his columns are in position.
6. Dillion's Right Column follows d'Estaing against the Spring Hill redoubt.
7. De Steding's Left Column moves to the left of the first two columns and struggles to advance in the swamp just north of the road. British cannon and musket fire force his men to follow the road toward Spring Hill redoubt.
8. Lauren's Right Column, led by the 2nd South Carolina Continental Regiment, moves in behind the French columns and their momentum pushes some of them into Spring Hill redoubt.
9. McIntosh's Left Column moves too far left (north) of de Steding's column and becomes isolated in the swamp. They retreat out of the fight having come under intense shipboard cannon fire.
10. As the French and American attack columns lose cohesion at the redoubt ditch, the British 60th Grenadiers and Royal Marines counterattack.
11. De Noailles' Reserve Column advances far enough from the Jewish cemeteries to thwart any further advance of the counter attack.

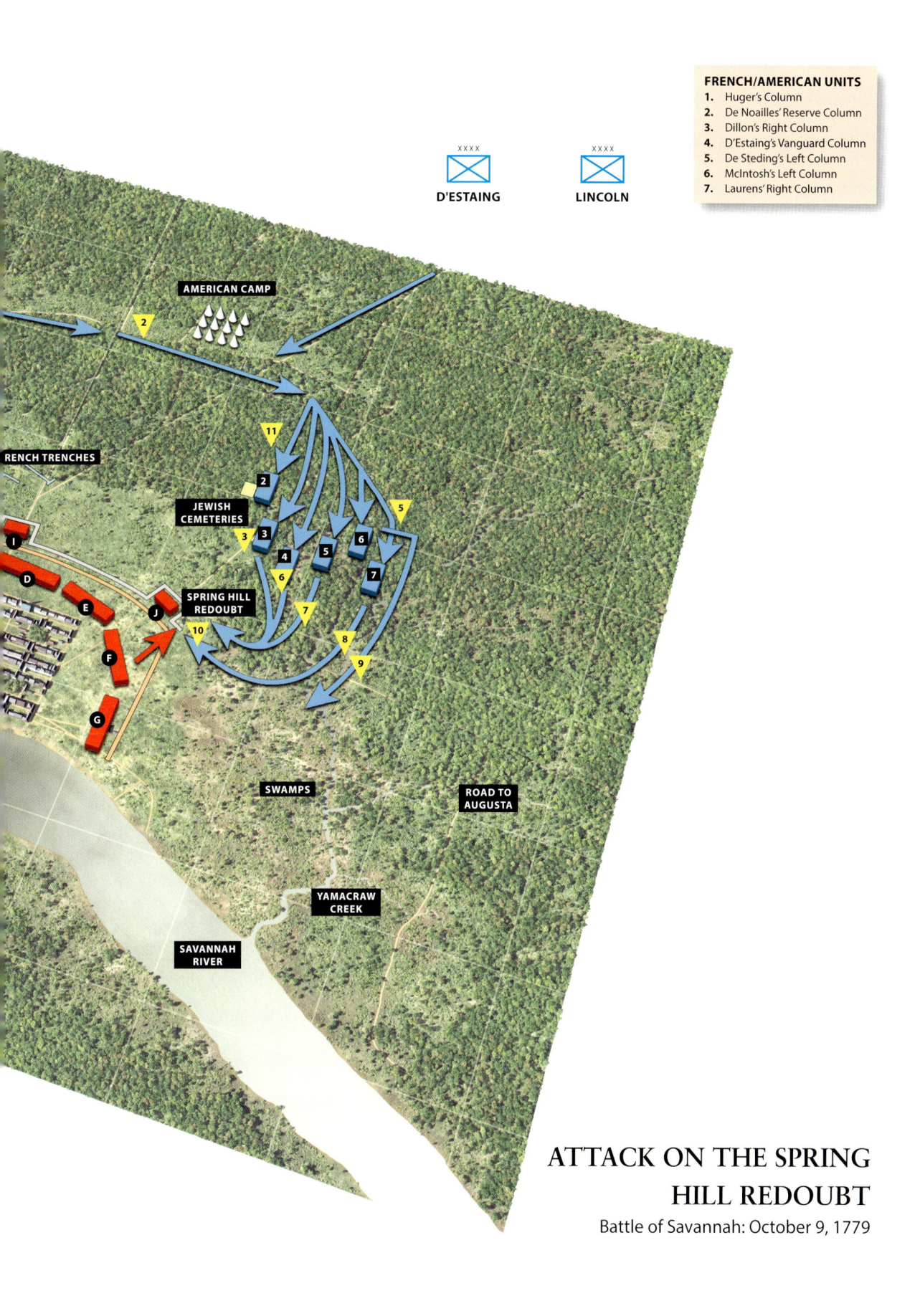

FRENCH/AMERICAN UNITS
1. Huger's Column
2. De Noailles' Reserve Column
3. Dillon's Right Column
4. D'Estaing's Vanguard Column
5. De Steding's Left Column
6. McIntosh's Left Column
7. Laurens' Right Column

D'ESTAING

LINCOLN

AMERICAN CAMP

FRENCH TRENCHES

JEWISH CEMETERIES

SPRING HILL REDOUBT

SWAMPS

ROAD TO AUGUSTA

YAMACRAW CREEK

SAVANNAH RIVER

ATTACK ON THE SPRING HILL REDOUBT
Battle of Savannah: October 9, 1779

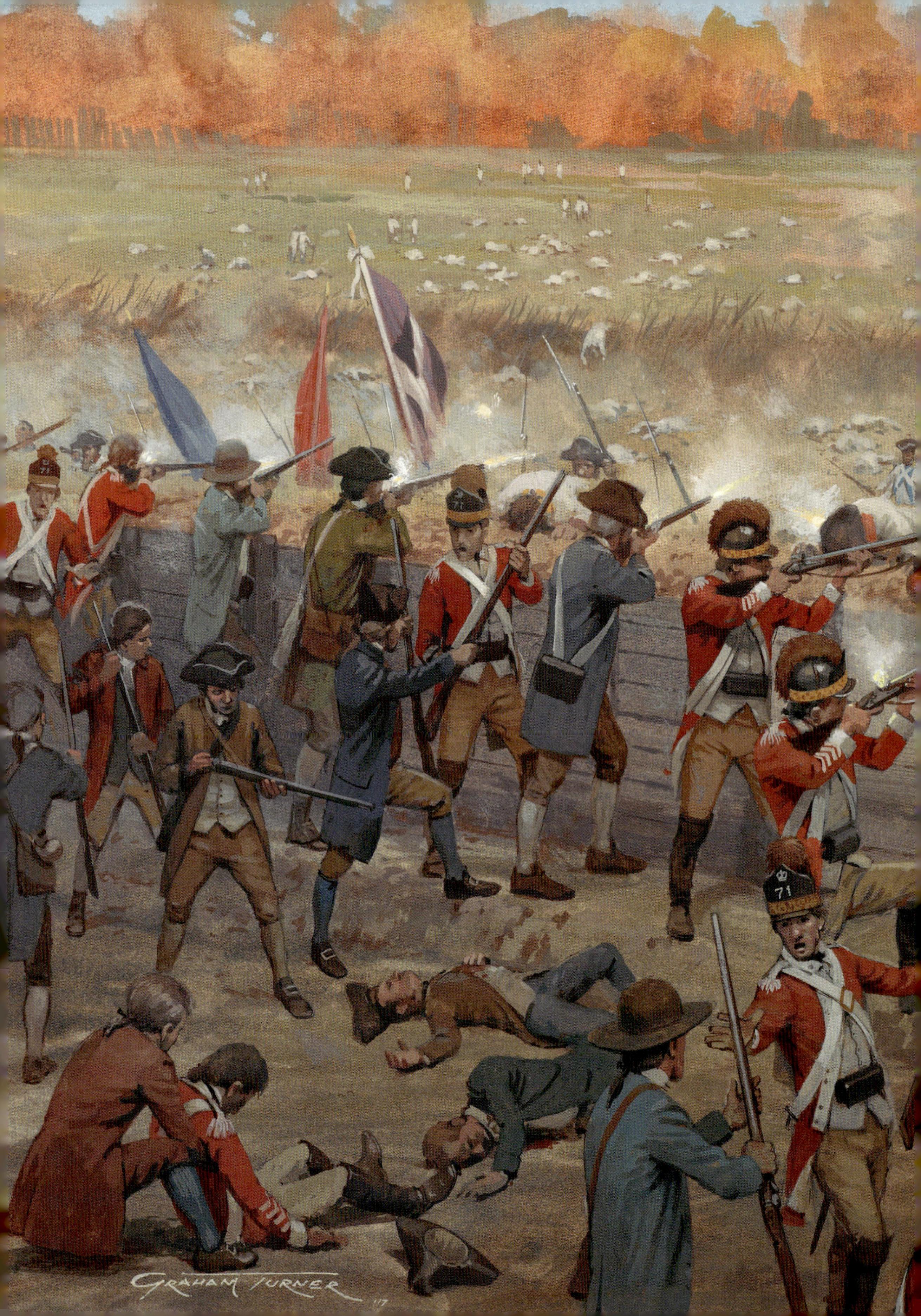
GRAHAM TURNER

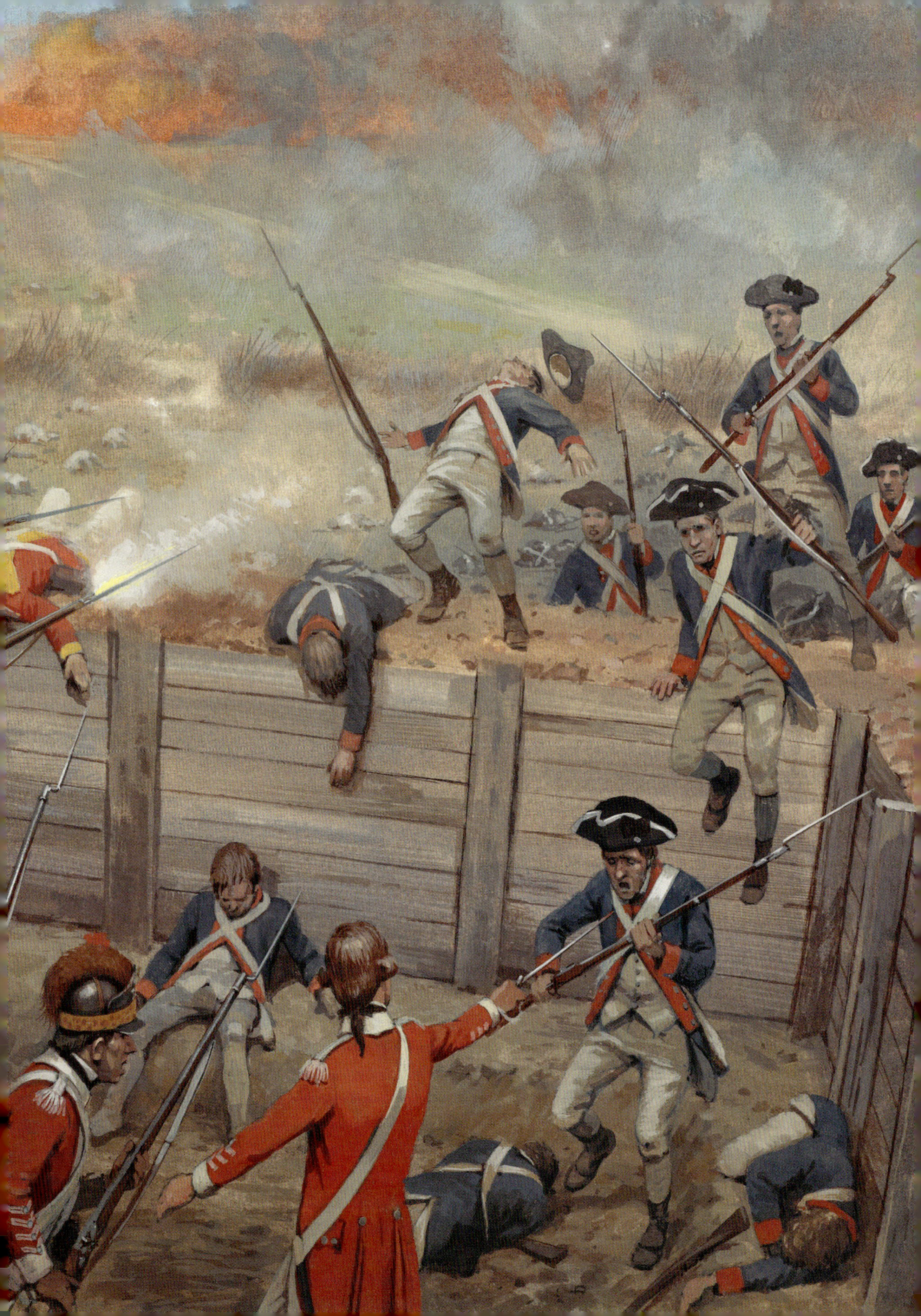

THE DEFENSE OF THE SPRING HILL REDOUBT, OCTOBER 9, 1779 (PP 84–85)

Spring Hill Redoubt was defended by 110 men under the command of Captain Thomas Tawes **(1)**. His force consisted of the 28 men from his dragoon force **(2)**, 28 men from the 4th Battalion 60th Regiment and 54 South Carolina loyalists **(3)**. Captain Tawes single-handedly steadied the Loyalists against the first two attacking columns by holding his sabre and yelling at them to hold firm and delivery a continuous fire into the French columns. As the focus of the attack centered on the northwest face of the redoubt, the defenders contracted their front to allow the third rank to reload for the first two ranks. As the American column entered the maelstrom, they were able to plant the 2nd South Carolina Continental flags **(4)** on the parapet as a small number of them were able to push their way into the redoubt. The painting shows the high point of the assault, with a mixed force of Continentals and French coming over the northwest corner of the parapet **(5)** while Captain Tawes is in a personal duel with a Continental soldier, two vanquished enemies at his feet. Tawes was killed later in the action.

they noticed the reserve column approaching from the Jewish cemetery. The counterattack was soon recalled as the French reserve column and men from the Chasseurs-Volontaires de Saint-Domingue advanced and delivered a volley fire from the column's front ranks. Prior to the counterattack, the second American column led by McIntosh, played a minor role in the attack as McIntosh marched his column farther to the left of the attacking columns and through the swampy ground to the right of the Carolina redoubt. Loyalist fire from the redoubt, coupled with cannon and shipboard fire, forced McIntosh's column to withdraw, effectively out of the fight.

As the firing stopped, the field in front of the Spring Hill and Carolina redoubts was a scene of carnage most had never seen before or would ever see again. A British soldier recounted the aftermath, "the ditch was filled with allied dead, many hung dead and wounded on the abatis, and outside the lines the plain was strewed with mangled bodies." General Huger's feint on the British left ended quickly as his 500 men, having struggled through the swampy rice fields and reached dry ground, were hit by a well-directed volley fire from the defenders. His men then turned and expeditiously retreated through the rice fields, leaving behind 28 men.

The French casualties were an appalling 61 officers and 760 men along with the Americans' loss of 312 men, whereas the British casualties amounted to 103 men. The one-hour battle resulted in the second-highest number of casualties suffered for the Patriot cause during the entire war. Several hours later, the two sides agreed to observe a four-hour truce to collect and bury the dead and retrieve their wounded. General Prevost summarized the losses in his dispatches:

> Our loss on this occasion was one captain, and fifteen rank and file killed, one captain, three subalterns, and thirty-five rank and file wounded. That of the enemy we do not exaggerate when we set it down from 1000 to 1200 killed and wounded. We buried within and near the abatis [Spring Hill redoubt] 203 on the right [northwest side], on the left 28 [southwest side], and delivered 116 wounded prisoners, the great part mortally. They themselves, by permission, buried those who lay more distant. Many no doubt were self-buried in the mud of the swamp, and many carried off.

The Levi Sheftall Cemetery, one of the two adjacent Jewish cemeteries designated as the rally point if the attack failed and position for the reserve column. (Congregation Mickve Israel)

As the two allied commanders took stock of their losses and considered their next move, the British were buoyed by their victory and waited for another assault. On October 10, Lincoln wrote to Governor Rutledge about the defeat and made note: "It cannot be doubted that if Great Britain is reinforced they will attack the place [Charles Town]." Lincoln argued for continuing the siege, but d'Estaing, dismayed by his horrendous losses from the failed attack and concern for his fleet, ordered a withdrawal. Lincoln later commented, "no argument could dissuade the count." By October 13, Lincoln and d'Estaing signed a mutual agreement to conduct an orderly retreat. The American army would withdraw after the evacuation of the wounded. The French began to dismantle their siege works, and transport their cannons, mortars, sick, and wounded to the landing sites at Thunderbolt Bluff and Causton's Bluff. By October 18, Lincoln's army vacated their camps and reached Zubley's Ferry that evening, crossing the Savannah River and back into Purysburg, South

Carolina two days later. Following the American departure, the remaining French infantry regiments, after covering the American withdrawal, marched to Thunderbolt Bluff and embarked on their ships. D'Estaing ordered Count de Grasse's squadron to resume its assignment in the West Indies; he had some ships sail into the Chesapeake Bay for repairs and the remainder would return to France with him. Prevost was content to wait behind his lines and observe the two armies' withdrawal, thereby enabling him to maintain control of Savannah and many counties of South Georgia.

Upon getting word of the battle at Savannah, General Clinton said of Prevost's victory, "I think this is the greatest event that has happened in the whole war." On October 29, Royal Governor Wright proclaimed a day of thanksgiving for the British victory. In addition to the fighting spirit of the British, German, and Loyalist soldiers, Prevost acknowledged the British commissary for surpassing all expectations. They had ensured Savannah was well stocked with provisions to support the size of Prevost's force and civilians for a considerable period of time. Prevost also noted that the quantity of provisions were never in doubt during the siege. Many of these provisions were obtained during the South Carolina expedition earlier in the spring and summer, as well as foraging details that had been sent throughout southeastern Georgia. Wright also wrote to Lord Germain following the battle praising Moncrief, "Give me leave to mention the great ability of Captain Moncrief, the Chief Engineer who was Indefatigable day & Night and whose Eminent Services contributed vastly to our defence and safety."

Although the British campaign to capture Savannah was a success, Prime Minister Lord North and George Germain appear not to have appreciated the significant impact it had on their southern strategy. The two issues overlooked by the victory were the British Navy's inability to control the American coast and the lack of loyalist support needed to help pacify Georgia and South Carolina. Although these factors would surface again, the firm control of Savannah provided General Clinton with a base of operations he could utilize for his 1780 campaign into South Carolina.

An early-morning assault by American and French forces on the Spring Hill redoubt. The illustration captures the intensity of the final assault on the redoubt. (National Archives)

AFTERMATH

On November 10 news reached Philadelphia of the Allied defeat at Savannah. Continental congressional delegates immediately placed blame on the French, whereas others placed it on General Lincoln. However, General Washington counseled Lincoln in various dispatches with the full understanding of the challenges he faced within the Southern Department and was clear to praise the behavior of Lincoln's troops and the delicacy and propriety of Lincoln's conduct with his French allies. Washington conveyed his support for Lincoln to Congress, which kept him in command of the Southern Department. To further add to Lincoln's problems for his defeated and demoralized army, smallpox broke out in Charles Town in November, and his army was forced to encamp outside the city, following its march from Purysburg. Many of his militia, fearful of catching the disease, returned to their homes and the rest of Lincoln's army eventually encamped on the 3,000-acre plantation belonging to former South Carolina Royal Governor William Bull Jr, near Sheldon, South Carolina for its winter quarters. It would remain in that area until late January 1780 under the command of Lieutenant-Colonel Marion. By early December, Marion reported to Lincoln, "Distress of the Soldiers, for want of Shoes, they are without & doing Duty in the field, Exceeding Cold & frost." Marion kept the men busy by erecting huts of logs and earth and sending small frequent parties of men across the river to ascertain the intentions of the British garrison in Savannah.

On December 26, General Clinton's army of 7,600 men sailed from New York City with the objective of capturing Charles Town. Winter storms off the Carolina coast scattered Admiral Arbuthnot's fleet of escort ships, 90 transport ships, and sank 14 vessels, some of which carried cavalry horses. Notwithstanding the weather, many

Henri Christophe, future King of Haiti and first African head of State in the Americas, served as a young drummer boy with the Chasseurs-Volontaires de Saint-Domingue during the siege. (Anne S.K. Brown Military Collection)

Jean-Baptiste Jourdan, a future Marshal of France under Napoleon Bonaparte, but in 1779 he was a 16-year-old assigned to the Auxerrois Regiment. Throughout his life, he would complain of the chronic illness, probably malaria, he suffered as a result of serving in the Caribbean under d'Estaing. (Anne S.K. Brown Military Collection)

of the ships arrived off Tybee Island by the end of January, which had been predetermined as the rendezvous location for the fleet. By February 10, the fleet consolidated and sailed to South Carolina. The next day, the fleet anchored off John's Island some 30 miles from Charles Town to begin offloading Clinton's army. Following three months of skirmishes and defending Charles Town against a siege, General Lincoln on May 12, 1780 surrendered the South Carolina capital and 5,400 men in the largest surrender of American forces during the entire war. Many of the soldiers were veterans of the October 9 assault on Savannah.

THE BATTLEFIELD TODAY

SPRING HILL REDOUBT MEMORIAL PARK

The memorial is dedicated to the soldiers and civilians of both sides who lost their lives during the Siege of Savannah. Admission is free and it is located in downtown Savannah, GA on the northwest side of the city in the famous Savannah historic district. The memorial field consists of a redoubt, along with markers on the ground west of the redoubt, donated by various organizations displaying the names of prominent people and events during the siege. A corner of the redoubt is visible. The memorial field is flat, similar to conditions during the assault, with markers in the ground to give visitors an idea of the size of a French or American assault column advancing toward the redoubt. The open-air memorial is located across the street from the Savannah History Museum. A final point of interest is Forsyth Park, a few blocks away, which was the location of the French camps and approaching trenches during the siege.

FORT MORRIS

Fort Morris State Historic Site is located 7 miles east of I-95 exit 76, via the Island Highway and Fort Morris road. The town of Sunbury no longer exists except for the cemetery, but portions of the fort's earthen wall still exist, sitting on the southern bank of the Medway River. A visitor center is open Thursday–Saturday from 9.00am to 5.00pm.

BELOW LEFT
Today's view of an attacking column heading toward the Spring Hill redoubt replica; each tablet on the ground represents a soldier. (Photograph by Scott Martin)

BELOW RIGHT
The replica of the Spring Hill redoubt as seen from the point of view of the attacker. D'Estaing's plan the night before the assault did not provide ample time for his men to construct ladders to help scale the steep parapet walls. (Photograph by Scott Martin)

Portion of the Fort Morris embankments seen today overlooking the Medway River. The original fort was star shaped and held a barracks within its walls. (Photograph by Scott Martin)

KETTLE CREEK

The battlefield is situated in a heavily wooded and hilly part of Wilkes County between the towns of Union Point and Washington, Georgia along route 44. A marker is located on the intersection of route 44 and route 68, indicating where you need to turn to visit the battlefield. Admission is free and the markers and plaques erected by the Daughters of the American Revolution and the Georgia Historical Society are to educate the public about the events which took place on this hallowed ground. In the center of these plaques is a small cemetery, which illustrates the significance of the site.

BRIER CREEK

The Brier Creek Battlefield is located about 10 miles northeast of Sylvania, Georgia. There is no cost for visiting the park, which is managed by Tuckahoe Wildlife Management. The park is heavily wooded with thick undergrowth and no walking paths. The memorial markers erected by the Georgia Historical Society and the Masonic Grand Lodge of Georgia are located in a small park right next to the bank of Brier Creek. Both markers provide a fair amount of detail on the battle, to give a visitor a good idea of the events surrounding the battle. However it is advisable to bring a healthy amount of mosquito repellant to avoid simulating actual battlefield conditions, if you plan to stay for an hour or more, even in December.

STONO FERRY

The entire battlefield of Stono Ferry has been absorbed into the limits of Hollywood, South Carolina about 10 miles southeast of Charleston. Visitors can drive to the "Links at Stono Ferry" golf course just south of route 162 in Hollywood and ask to visit the 12th hole where a battlefield marker is currently on display just north of the Stono River. From this vantage point a visitor can imagine the hastily dug earthworks and moss-covered trees, as flags and the sound of drums and bagpipes filled the morning air.

Portion of the Brier Creek battlefield depicting the wooded area the 71st would have encountered as it deployed from a road column into its line of battle. (Photograph by Bernard Harris)

FURTHER READING

Anderson, Chase and Tudor, Christine, "October 9, 1779 – the French supporting the American Independence attempt to defeat the British in Savannah" in *Cross Cultural Comments and History* (October 9, 2010)

Boulware, Tyler, "Cherokee Indians." *New Georgia Encyclopedia,* 19 October 2016.

Brown, Wallace, *The Good Americans: The Loyalists in the American Revolution,* William Morrow and Company, Inc. (1969)

Campbell, Archibald (edited by Colin Campbell), *Journal of An Expedition against the Rebels of Georgia in North America Under the orders of Archibald Campbell Esquire Lieut. Colol. of His Majesty's 71st Regimt, 1778,* Ashantilly Press (1981)

Carrington, Henry B., *Battles of the American Revolution 1775–1781,* Promontory Press, New York (originally published 1877)

Carrington, Henry B., *Battles of the American Revolution; Battle Maps and Charts of the American Revolution,* The New York Times and Arno Press (1877)

Cashin, Edward J., "Revolutionary War in Georgia." *New Georgia Encyclopedia,* 11 October 2016.

Chartrand, René, *The French Army in the American War of Independence,* Osprey Publishing Ltd (2002)

Chartrand, René, *American Loyalist Troops 1775–84,* Osprey Publishing Ltd (2008)

Coates, Earl J. and Kochan, James L., *Don Troiani's Soldiers in America 1754–1865,* Stackpole Books (1998)

Davis, Robert S., "Change and Remembrance: How Promoting the Kettle Creek Battlefield went from the Means to Becoming the End in Itself" in *Journal of the Georgia Association of Historians* 24 (2003)

Dull, Jonathan R., *The French Navy and American Independence,* Princeton University Press (1975)

Edgar, Walter, *Partisans and Redcoats: The Southern Conflict that Turned the Tide of The American Revolution,* Harper Collins (2001)

Elliot, Daniel T., *Archaeological Investigations at Fort Morris State Historic Site, Liberty County, Georgia,* Georgia Department of Natural Resources Parks and Historic Sites Division (2003)

Elliot, Daniel T., *Stirring Up a Hornet's Nest: The Kettle Creek Battlefield Survey,*

Lamar Institute Publication Series, Report Number 131, The Lamar Institute, Inc. (2008)

Furlong, Patrick J., *Civilian–Military Conflict and the Restoration of the Royal Province of Georgia 1778–1782,* Cambridge University Press (1972)

Golden, Randy, *The Siege and Battle of Savannah,* Our Georgia History, Golden Ink (2001–2014)

Golden, Randy, *The First Florida Expedition,* Our Georgia History, Golden Ink (2001–2014)

Gordon, John W., *South Carolina and The American Revolution: A Battlefield History,* University of South Carolina Press (2003)

Hibbert, Christopher, *Redcoats and Rebels,* W.W. Norton and Company, Inc. (1990)

Jackson, Harvey H., *The Battle of the Riceboats: Georgia Joins the Revolution,* Georgia Historical Quarterly (1974)

Johnson, Daniel McDonald, *Brier Creek Battleground: An illustrated guide to a Revolutionary War site beside the Savannah River,* private publication (2014)

Jones, Charles C. (editor), *The Siege of Savannah by the Fleet of Count D'Estaing in 1779,* Arno Press, Inc. (1968)

Kennett, Lee, *The French Forces in America, 1780–1783,* Greenwood Press, Inc. (1977)

May, Robin, *The British Army in North America,* Osprey Publishing Ltd (1974)

Moebs, Thomas Truxton, *Black Soldiers – Black Sailors – Black Ink,* Moebs Publishing Co. (1994)

Moultrie, William, *Memoirs of the American Revolution so far as it relates to The States of North and South Carolina, and Georgia,* The New York Times and Arno Press (1968)

Lumpkin, Henry, *From Savannah to Yorktown – The American Revolution in the South,* University of South Carolina Press (1981)

Mattern, David B., *Benjamin Lincoln and The American Revolution,* University of South Carolina Press (1995)

Mollo, John, *Uniforms of The American Revolution,* Sterling Publishing Co., Inc., New York (1991)

Morrill, Dr. Dan L., *Southern Campaign of The American Revolution,* The Nautical and Aviation Publishing Company of America (1996)

Morrissey, Brendan, *Monmouth Courthouse 1778,* Osprey Publishing Ltd (2004)

Peter, Courtney, "Come And Take It! – Rallying Cry of Revolutionaries" in *American Spirit* magazine: Daughters of the American Revolution, November/December 2015 edition

Russell, David Lee, *The American Revolution in the Southern Colonies*, McFarland and Company, Inc., Publishers (2000)

Scheer, George F. and Rankin, Hugh F., *Rebels and Redcoats: The American Revolution Through the Eyes of Those Who Fought and Lived It*, The World Publishing Company (1957)

Searcy, Martha Condray, *The Georgia–Florida Contest in the American Revolution, 1776–1778*, The University of Alabama Press (1985)

Sheely, Horace J. Jr, *Siege of Savannah Battle Site, 1779*, National Park Service (NP) (September 9, 1965)

Sheftall, John McKay, *Sunbury on the Medway*, The Georgia Department of Natural Resources (1995)

Siry, Steve E., *Liberty's Fallen Generals: Leadership and Sacrifice in the American War of Independence*, Potomoc Books, Inc., Washington, DC (2012)

Smith, David, *Camden 1780: The Annihilation of Gates' Grand Army*, Osprey Publishing Ltd (2016)

Smith, Digby and Kiel, Kevin, *An Illustrated Encyclopedia of Uniforms of The American War of Independence 1777–1783*, Lorenz Books (2011)

Smith, Gordon Burns, "Siege of Savannah" in *New Georgia Encyclopedia* (September, 2013)

Smith, Gordon Burns, *Morningstars of Liberty: The Revolutionary War in Georgia 1775–1783*, Volume 1, Boyd Publishing (2006)

Spring, Matthew H., *With Zeal and With Bayonets only: The British Army on campaign in North America, 1775–1783*, University of Oklahoma: Norman (2010)

Swisher, James K., *The Revolutionary War in the Southern Back Country*, Pelican Publishing Company (2008)

Weeks, Carl Solana, *Savannah in the Time of Peter Tondee*, Summerhouse Press (1997)

Wilson, David K., *The Southern Strategy: Britain's Conquest of South Carolina and Georgia, 1775–1780*, University of South Carolina Press (2005)

Wright, Robert K., *Army Lineage Series: The Continental Army*, Center of Military History, United States Army (1983)

INDEX

Page numbers in **bold** refer to illustrations and their captions.

African forces 19, 60, 78, 87, **89**
Allen, Colonel Isaac 45
American forces
    battle orders 23–24
    commanders 10–12
    overview 16–18
    plans 25–28
American units
    Charles Town militia 80
    Georgia Brigade 16–17, **38–39**, 40, 53, 56
    Georgia militia 17–18, 26, 27–28, 34–35, 37–40, **38–39**, 47–48
    North Carolina Brigade 17, 48, 51–53, 56, 62–66, **64–65**
    North Carolina (Edenton) militia 53, 56, 62–66, **64–65**
    Pulaski's legion 12, 59, 78, 81
    South Carolina Brigade 17, **38–39**, 40, 41, 62–66, **64–65**, 68, 78, 80, **82–83**
    South Carolina militia 17–18, 26, 27, 47, 48, 49, 53, **61**, 62–66, **64–65**, 69
    South Carolina Ninety-Six Militia Regiment 18, 50–51
    Virginia Brigade 80
artillery **51**, **54–55**, 76
Ashe, Brigadier-General John 51–53, 56
Augusta
    expedition to 46–48, **47**
    geography 7

Baird, Captain Sir James 36, 40
Beaufort 48–49, **58**, 66, 67
Beaulieu Plantation **69**, 70, 72
Béthisy, Colonel Jules 78
Boyd, Colonel John 50–51
Brétigny, Colonel Charles-François Sevelinges, Marquis de 67
Brier Creek, battle of (1779)
    action **47**, 52–53, **54–55**
    battle orders 23
    memorials 92, **92**
British forces
    battle orders 23–24
    commanders 13–15
    overview 19–22
    plans 31–32
British units
    16th Regiment of Foot 20, 45–46, 48–49, **75**, 79, 81–87
    60th Regiment 20, 45–46, 48–49, 52, 57–58, 79, **82–83**, **84–85**
    71st Highland Regiment 20, **20**, 33, 37, **38–39**, 40, 46, 51–53, **54–55**, 62–66, **64–65**, 67–68, 69–70, 72–73, 75, 79, 81, **82–83**
    Baird's Light Infantry 46, 51–53
    Carolina Cavalry 48
    DeLancey's Brigade (New York Loyalists) **21**, 22, 33, 37, **38–39**, 40, 46, 51–52, 57–58, 68–70, 79, **82–83**
    East Florida Rangers (King's Rangers) 22, 45–46, 47, 48, 51–53, **82–83**
    Ebenezer Battery 79
    Georgia Loyalists 79
    Hessian Regiment von Trumbach (previously von Woellwarth) **20**, 21–22, 33, **38–39**, 40, 46, 67, 79, **82–83**
    Hessian Regiment von Wissenbach 22, 33, 40, 46, 62–63, **64–65**, 67, 79, **82–83**
    New Jersey Volunteers 22, 33, 36, 45–46, 67
    North Carolina Loyalists 50–51, 52–53, 62–66, **64–65**, 79, **82–83**
    Royal Marines **20**, 79, 81–87, **82–83**
    South Carolina Loyalists 45–46, 47, 51–52, 62–66, **64–65**, 79, **84–85**
    Tawes' dragoons 20, 46, 52–53, 59, 79–80, **82–83**, **84–85**
Brown, Lieutenant-Colonel Thomas "Burnfoot" 22, 47
Broyes, Count de 72, 74
Bull, Brigadier Stephen 49
Burke County Jail 47
Byron, Admiral 30

Cameron, Captain 37
Campbell, Lieutenant-Colonel Archibald 15, **42–43**
    on American militia 18
    and Augusta expedition 46–48, 50, 51
    background 14–15
    campaign orders 33
    cavalry force raised by 20
    hands over command and goes home 51–52, 53
    on Hessian troops 20
    and prisoner exchange 46
    and Savannah 36, 37, 40, 41–45
    voyage to Georgia 33, **34**
Carlisle, Lord 5
Carr's Fort 50
Charles Town (Charleston) 7, **31**
    American preparations to defend 67–68
    British expedition to 57–61, **58**
    captured by British 89–90
Clarke, Lieutenant-Colonel Elijah 50–51
Clinton, Lieutenant-General Henry **13**
    background 13
    campaign orders 33
    Charles Town captured by 89–90
    objectives 5
    on Savannah (1779) 88
    on Stuart 31
    and Sullivan Island 31
Cruger, Lieutenant-Colonel John 67, 69–70

DeLancy, Oliver 22
Dillon, Count Arthur 78
Dooley, Colonel John 50

East Florida
    American attempts to capture 25–28, **26**
    Loyalist families moving to 34
Ebenezer 6–7, 45
Elbert, Colonel Samuel 16, 40, 47, 53, 56
equipment *see* weapons and equipment
Erskine, Sir William 20
Estaing, Vice-Admiral Charles-Henri, Count d' **12**
    background 12
    and Newport and Caribbean 12, 28–31, **29**
    and Savannah (1779) 67, 68, 71–74, 75, 76–78, 79–82, 87–88
    on US militia 18
Experiment, HMS 74, 75

Florida *see* East Florida
Fontanges, Viscount François de 68, 71, 77, 80
Fort George (previously Morris) 35, **40**, 46, 91, **92**
Fort Henderson 47–48
Fort Savannah **42–43**
Fort Sullivan 16, 31
Franklin, Benjamin 6, 12
French forces 78
    battle orders 23–24
    commanders 12
    overview 18–19
    plans 28–31
French units
    Chasseurs-Volontaires de Saint-Domingue 19, 60, 78, 87, **89**
    Dillon's regiment 19, 78, 79–80, **82–83**
    Gatinois Regiment 19
    Walsh's regiment 19
Fuser, Lieutenant-Colonel Lewis 35

Gadsden, Christopher 27, 28
Gadsden, Captain Thomas 68
Gadsden Flag 27
Gambier, Rear Admiral 33
Gardner, Major William 48–49
Garth, Brigadier-General George 67, 75
Germain, Lord *see* Sackville, George, Lord Germain
Glazier, Major Beamsley 45–46, 81–87
Graham, Major **75**
Grenada **29**, 30, 31
Gwinnett, Button 25, **26**, 27

Habersham, Major John 69
Habersham, Lieutenant-Colonel Joseph 68
Hamilton, Major John 50, 79
Hart, Nancy 49
Henderson, Lieutenant-Colonel 62
Henri Christophe, King of Haiti **89**
Heyward, Thomas **67**
Houston, John 27–28, 36, 37
Howe, Major-General Robert **10**
    and American attacks on East Florida 26, 27–28
    background 10
    Gadsden duel 28
    Georgian incursion 35–36
    relationship with colonial governors 16
    and Savannah 36–41
Huger, Brigadier Isaac
    background 11
    and Savannah (1778) 17, 40
    and Savannah (1779) 68, 78, 82, 87
    and Savannah campaign 57
    and Stono Ferry 62–63

Jackson, Hugh **66**
Jackson, Robert 66
Jameson, Major John 66

Jasper, Sergeant William 80, **81**
Jourdan, Jean-Baptiste 90

Kettle Creek, battle of (1779) 47, **48**, 50–51, 92

Lane, Major Joseph 46
Laurens, Lieutenant-Colonel John 58–59, 60, 78, 80, 82
Lee, General Charles 26
Lee, Colonel Henry "Light Horse Harry" 41
L'Enfant, Major Pierre Charles 77
Lincoln, Major-General Benjamin **11**
  almost retires 61–62
  appearance and background 10, 28
  and Brier Creek 52, 53
  and Charles Town expedition 58–59, 61
  Charles Town surrendered by 90
  and Port Royal Island 49
  and prisoner exchange 46
  and Savannah (1779), 68, 70–71, 72–73, 76–77, 78, 79, 87
  and Savannah campaign 36, 45, 51, 53–57, 66–67
  Savannah performance assessed 89
  and Stono Ferry 62–66
Louis XVI, King of France and Navarre 4, **5**, **6**

MacAlister, Private 48
MacArthur, Major 45, 75
McIntosh, Lieutenant-Colonel John 34, 35, 53, 56
McIntosh, Brigadier-General Lachlan **25**
  Gwinnett duel 27
  and Savannah (1779) 71, 78, 82, 87
McLeod, Captain Donald 31
Maitland, Lieutenant-Colonel John **15**
  background 15
  and Brier Creek 52
  and Charles Town expedition 57–58, 59
  and Savannah (1778) 37
  and Savannah (1779) 67–68, 69–70, 72–73
  and Stono Ferry 62–66
Malmady, Colonel Francis 63–66
Manly, Captain 79
Marion, Lieutenant-Colonel Francis 72, 80, 89
Martin, Josiah 31
Meade, Everard 57
Midway 34–35
Moncrief, Captain James
  background 15
  and Charles Town expedition 59
  Savannah defenses built by 70, 74, 75, 88
Monmouth Courthouse, battle of (1778) 5, 13
Moore's Creek, battle of (1776) 31
Morris, Captain Thomas 69
Moultrie, Brigadier-General William **12**
  background 10–11, 16
  and Charles Town defenses 68–69
  and Charles Town expedition 58–61
  on Howe at Savannah 41
  and Port Royal Island 49
  and Savannah campaign 57, 67

on Spring Hill redoubt attack 81
and Stono Ferry 62–63

Native Americans
  American attempts to keep from British service 53, 57
  in British service 34, 57–58, 76
  British treatment 31
  as threat to Americans in the backcountry 25, 26
  trade center 7
Newport, Rhode Island 12, 28–31, **29**
Noailles, General Louis Marie de 78, 82

O'Connor, Captain Antoine 74, 77

Parker, Commodore Hyde 33, 36, 37
Parker, Colonel Richard 66
Pickens, Colonel Andrew 18, 50–51
Pinckney, Major Thomas 46, 68, 71
Porbeck, Colonel von 79
Port Royal Island, skirmish at (1779) 47, **48**–49
Prevost, Anne 76
Prevost, Major-General Augustine **14**
  background 14
  and Beaufort 48–49
  campaign orders 33, 36
  and Charles Town expedition 57, 58–62
  and Loyalist troops 22, 32
  and prisoners of war 46
  resigns 67
  and Savannah (1779) 67, 68, 69–70, 72–73, 76, 79, 87, 88
  and Savannah campaign 52, 66
  and Sunbury 34, 45–46
Prevost, Lieutenant-Colonel James
  Campbell's command given to 15, 51, 52
  and Charles Town expedition 60
  as Georgia's interim governor 52
  at Stono Ferry bridgehead 62
  Sunbury provisioning expedition 34–35
prisoners of war 46, 51, 69
Pulaski, Brigadier-General Count Casimir **12**
  background 11–12
  and Charles Town expedition 59, 60, 61
  and Savannah (1779) 80, 81
Purysburg 45, 53, 57–58, 58

Rice Boats, Battle of the (1776) 25
Roberts, Colonel Owen 62–63, 66
Robinson, Lieutenant-Colonel Thomas 47
Rochambeau, Count de 12
Rutledge, Captain Edward 53
Rutledge, Governor John 59
  attempt to negotiate neutrality with British 60
  and Charles Town defenses 59, 66, 69, 87
  and Jasper 81
  and Lincoln's attempted resignation 61–62
  plantation plundered by British 62

Sackville, George, Lord Germain 5, 13, 33, 67, 88

St Augustine **7**
  American attempts to capture 10, 25–28
  British garrison 45–46
  Loyalist families moving to 34
St Lucia 31
St Vincent **28**, **29**, 31
Savannah **6**
  Brewton's Bluff **36**, 37, **37**
  Levi Sheftall Cemetery **87**
  strategic importance and geography 5–6
Savannah, battle of (1778) 23, **34**, 36–41, **42–43**
Savannah, battle of (1779)
  battle orders 23–24
  bombardment 76–78, **76**
  Carolina redoubt assault 78, 79, 87
  memorials to **91**
  preparations 67–74, **68**, **69**
  Spring Hill redoubt assault 71, 77–87, **77**, **79**, **82–83**, **84–85**, **88**, **91**
Screven, Brigadier-General James 34–35
Skelly, Major Francis John 40, 57–58, 60
slaves and slavery 6, 13, 66, 70, 76
Smith, Captain 37, 38
Spurgeon, Major William 51
Stark, General John 12
Steding, Baron de 78, 80, 82
Stiel, Captain 79
Stirk, Colonel John 69
Stokes, Anthony 76
Stono Ferry, battle of (1779) 23, 62–66, **64–65**, 92
Stuart, John 31, 36
  home **31**
Sullivan, General John 12, 28–31
Sullivan Island *see* Fort Sullivan
Sumner, General Jethro 57, 62–63
Sunbury 6, 34–36, **40**, 45–46, 68, 91, 92

Tawes, Captain Thomas 20, 52, 79, 80, **84–85**
Thompson, Colonel William 40
Tondee, Lucy 41
Tonyn, Patrick 22, **32**, 36

uniforms
  American **17**
  British 20, **20**, **21**, 22
  French 19, **19**

Walton, Colonel George 45, 69
Washington, George 28, 89
weapons and equipment
  muskets **18**, 20
  powder horns **41**
White, Colonel John 34–35
Williamson, General Andrew 27–28, 48, 53
Wright, Sir James **14**
  background 13–14, 25
  British attempt to reinstate in Georgia 36, 52
  reinstated 67
  and Savannah (1779) 70, 76, 88
Wright, Major James (son of the above) 14